*R. D. Bartlett and
Patricia P. Bartlett*

Snakes

Everything about Selection,
Care, Nutrition, Diseases,
Breeding, and Behavior

With 104 Color Photographs

Illustrations by Michele Earle-Bridges
and David Wenzel

BARRON'S

About the Authors

R. D. Bartlett is a herpetologist and herpetoculturist who has authored more than 425 articles and three books and coauthored an additional 11 books. He lectures extensively and has participated in field studies across North and Latin America. Bartlett is a member of numerous herpetological and conservation organizations, a co-host on an "on-line" reptile and amphibian forum, and a contributing editor of *Reptiles Magazine*.

Patricia Bartlett is a biologist and historian who has authored 5 books and coauthored 11 books. A museum administrator for the last 15 years, she has worked in both history and science museums.

In 1970, the Bartletts began the Reptilian Breeding and Research Institute (RBRI), a private facility. Since its inception, more than 200 species of reptiles and amphibians have been bred at RBRI, some for the first time in the United States under captive conditions. Successes at the RBRI include several endangered species.

All inquiries should be addressed to:
Barron's Educational Series, Inc.
250 Wireless Boulevard
Hauppauge, NY 11788

International Standard Book No. 0-7641-0055-6

Library of Congress Catalog Card No. 97-29243

Library of Congress Cataloging-in-Publication Data
Bartlett, Richard D., 1938–
    Snakes / R.D. Bartlett and Patricia P. Bartlett.
        p.   cm. — (A complete pet owner's manual)
    Includes bibliographical references (p. 108) and index.
    ISBN 0-7641-0055-6
    1. Snakes as pets. 2. Snakes. I. Bartlett, Patricia Pope, 1949–. II. Title. III. Series.
SF459.S5B376   1998
639.3′96—dc21   97-29243
                                                        CIP

Printed in Hong Kong

987

639.396
BART

3 2530 60577 2837

Acknowledgments

To Rob MacInnes of Glades, Herp, Inc., Chris McQuade of Gulf Coast Reptiles, (Ft. Myers, FL), to Bill Love of Blue Chameleon Ventures (Alva, FL), Regis Opferman (Pueblo, CO), and Kenny Wray (Arlington, TX), we extend thanks for the photographic opportunities. Bill Griswold (Hogwild, Spring Hill, FL) and Billy Griswold (Next Generation Herpetoculture, Gainesville, FL), unhesitatingly provided us with information regarding their breeding programs for hog-nosed snakes and rough green snakes. Bill Brant (The Gourmet Rodent of Gainesville, FL) afforded me the opportunity to photograph his brown house snakes, and Carl May shared with me some of his experiences with both brown house snakes and rainbow boas. John Decker provided more than marginal insight into his breeding programs with his favored rosy and Keys variant rat snakes.

A note of thanks is due Doug Wagner for his critical evaluation of, and pertinent contributions to, our manuscript as well as to our editor, Mark Miele, for guiding us along the intricate pathways leading to publication.

Photo Credits

All photos by R.D. Bartlett except for the following: photos on pages 29 bottom, 48 top and bottom, 65, 67 top right and bottom, 71, 77 top, 94, 95, 96, 105 by Bill Griswold; on pages 44, 45 top left, 46, 51 top, 56 by Zig Leszczynski; on page 92 bottom by Carl D. May.

Important Note
The subject of this book is the keeping and care of nonpoisonous snakes. Snake keepers should realize, however, that even the bite of a snake regarded as nonpoisonous can have harmful consequences. So see a doctor immediately after any snake bite.

Handling giant serpents requires a lot of experience and a great sense of responsibility. Carelessness can be deadly! Inexperienced snake keepers and snake keepers who have small children are therefore urgently advised not to keep giant serpents.

Electrical appliances used in the care of snakes must carry a valid "UL approved" marking. Everyone using such equipment should be aware of the dangers involved with it. It is strongly recommended that you purchase a device that will instantly shut off the electrical current in the event of failure in the appliances or wiring. A circuit-protection device with a similar function has to be installed by a licensed electrician.

Contents

Preface

There has been such a proliferation of serpent-related knowledge in the last quarter century, that the burgeoning hobby of today is barely recognizable as the hobby we remember from the 70s (and before). Corn snakes, kingsnakes, gopher snakes, boas and pythons—all are being captive-bred in such numbers that it now seems they come from a bottomless pit. For example, there is a "captive-bred expo" in Orlando, Florida each August that brings together some 450 reptile-vendors (mostly of snakes) and 10,000 hobbyists in four auditorium-sized conference rooms. We marvel at this and compare the days of our childhoods when we felt gratified if we could find just a single other enthusiast with whom to share our experiences.

The immense popularity of snakes as pets may have a downside. Collecting pressures on wild snake populations continue to increase each year. Additionally, thousands upon thousands of snakes are killed on roadways and by humans who have not yet learned to appreciate these creatures of the wild. Increased predator populations (especially dogs, cats, raccoons and in the southern tier states, the fire ants), take an unknown, but probably *very* significant toll. It is unlikely that snake populations in some areas can sustain such unnatural pressures and remain viable much longer. If we hope to preserve the wild populations of many snakes for our and our children's enjoyment, we, as naturalists and hobbyists, must begin thinking and obeying practices of conservation.

In this book, we have tried to offer you an overview of the snake species most favored by American hobbyists. Most are also of interest to hobbyists elsewhere in the world. We hope that our comments on these pages will help you develop a greater interest and better understanding of the varied animals integral to the enjoyment of our hobby and to the success of the business of herpetoculture as we know it today.

Dick and Patti Bartlett

Captive Care

Choosing a Snake

Once a hobbyist decides to acquire a snake, the question then becomes, what kind would be best? The choices offered by even a small pet store can be overwhelming.

When deciding on a snake, numerous questions need to be asked. Some of the questions include how much room do you have for the terrarium, what will you feel most comfortable feeding the snake, can you maintain a constant tropical temperature or is a variable temperature more usual in your house, and do you want a captive bred or a wild collected specimen?

Why these questions?

Well, if you only have space for a 10-gallon terrarium, you certainly wouldn't want to buy a cribo or a Burmese python; the first of which could exceed a heavy-bodied 7 feet in length, while the Burmese could exceed more than 20 feet!

If you want to feed your snake worms or fish, neither a rat snake nor a kingsnake would be the correct choice.

If your winter indoor temperatures vary nearly as much as the outdoor temperatures, you should not consider a tropical emerald tree boa.

As regards the final question, it is less likely that a captive-bred and born or hatched snake will harbor as many endoparasites as a wild-collected specimen, but a captive-bred one *may* be a little more costly.

After reading this book, you may decide that a garter, brown, or rough green snake would all be good choices.

None are large, all eat worms, fish, or insects, all are from temperate climates and can withstand a reasonable degree of temperature fluctuation (including a period of winter hibernation, should you choose to provide it), and none are particularly costly—whether wild collected or captive reproduced.

On the other hand, if you have always dreamt of having a huge snake, have lots of room to devote to caging, don't mind feeding your snake rabbits and can afford to do so, and can provide a rather constant year-round temperature, a big boa or a Burmese python might be the perfect choice for you.

These are also discussed herein.

Rough green snakes are among the only insectivorous snake species commonly kept captive.

The time to make all of the decisions pertinent to snake keeping is *before* and not after your purchase. The proper decision will save you much unnecessary agonizing and ensure that you and your snake have an enjoyable, lengthy, relationship.

Caging and Keeping Suggestions

Most common pet snake species are undemanding animals. They require feeding perhaps once a week; some can fast for months without any deleterious effects. Fresh water (see the restrictions for the aridland snake species on p. 44) and adequately sized cages are easily supplied.

When deciding on caging, do not be deceived by a snake's common name. For example, although the members of the natricine genus *Nerodia* are called water snakes, they spend the better portion of their days (and all of their nights) on tree limbs, out of the water. Captives, when kept in an aquarium setup or even in an overly damp terrestrial terrarium where they cannot dry off, will develop skin lesions which can ultimately be fatal.

Because of the availability of commercial reptile cages, it is unnecessary to convert aquaria into terraria, although you certainly can do so.

The responsible snake owner will try to provide captive snakes the most naturalistic surroundings possible. We don't delude ourselves that we can recreate nature but we do try hard to make the snakes feel safe, secure, and at home. In our attempt to do this, cage furnishings figure prominently.

Cage furniture: This term describes virtually any and all cage decorations whether a simple wooden snag, an inverted cardboard hidebox, growing plant, or a plastic vine.

When providing a climbing surface or limbs, remember that most snakes seek the stability offered by firmly affixed, sizable limbs. The slender and almost feather-light rough green snake can be found in twigtips, but even it prefers the stability offered by vine tangles. Provide limbs one and a half times the diameter of your snake's body. You may either wedge the limbs firmly in place or glue exact lengths into place using aquarium sealant on the aquarium glass.

We also place heavy logs on the terrarium bottom. The snakes may rest on or behind them. Place the logs directly on the cage bottom (not atop the substrate) or secure them so that a burrowing snake can't be crushed under them.

Most snakes spend their time in hiding. By nature, snakes are secretive beasts, but some hide more persistently than others, especially during the daylight hours. Most captive snakes will use a hide box or other place of concealment. In fact, if forced to stay in the open, many snakes will become stressed and refuse to eat. This is especially true if the snake's cage is located in a heavily trafficked area and if the snake is one of the more nervous species.

A readily replaceable small cardboard box with an access hole cut in one side will suffice. Pet stores often

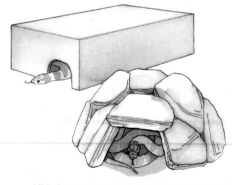

Hide boxes provide snakes with a needed feeling of security.

have preformed plastic "caves" and combination cave-water dishes. These are washable, sterilizable, and will last for years. We provide natural hollow limbs and hollowed cactus skeletons that are readily found in woods and fields. These can be used as floor furnishings or can be Silastic-secured at suitable levels in the terraria. Corkbark is a reasonable alternative to the hollow limbs and is much lighter, more impervious to body wastes, and easily cleaned and sterilized. It is available at many pet stores, reptile dealers, and plant nurseries. When the snake is getting ready to shed and its eyes turn "blue," its vision is impaired. It is then that snakes are even more secretive than usual.

Heating sources include incandescent bulbs, ceramic heating "coils," heating pads, and heating tapes. To provide a temperature gradient these are best situated in one end of the terrarium.

Lighting, Heating, and a Comment on Weather Patterns

Staying warm: Snakes are ectothermic creatures which use outside sources of heating and cooling to regulate their body temperatures. At most times snakes (which are secretive creatures) will warm themselves by basking in a secluded place.

Although tropical and semitropical snake species may remain active all year-round, northern snakes hibernate. Snakes in regions that are subject to periodic cold spells may become dormant only during those cold spells. Even though semiactive, these snakes may not feed for most of the cooler time of the year.

Staying cool: Although snakes vary in their adaptations, it is as important for snakes to remain comfortably cool as warm. During hot weather or where temperatures are naturally very hot (southwestern deserts), most snakes become nocturnal or aestivate (undergo a period of warm weather dormancy) through the weeks of excessive heat. Desert snakes may be diurnal during cool weather and nocturnal during the hot summers.

Thermoregulation is important even for captive snakes. They, of course, are dependent on us, their keepers, to provide them with caging that lets them select their optimum body temperature. Warming the cage may be done using heating pads or heating tapes. (Hot rocks are not recommended.) Ceramic heating units that screw in to a light socket and light bulbs (especially those with directed beams such as flood and spotlights) are other possible sources of heat, and the bulbs provide light. Try to maintain a "hot spot" temperature of 80–87°F. Fluorescent bulbs provide light but little heat, which can be advantageous when you live in a warmer area where additional heat is not needed.

Night temperatures should be cooler by several degrees than daytime temperatures (from 75–85°F).

Light: Natural light cycles are nearly as important as temperature. Under normal conditions, snake activity is greatest during the longest days of the year (which just happen to coincide with the most optimum temperatures as well). Snakes that hibernate will do so during the shortest (and coldest) days of the year.

Full-spectrum/ultraviolet light: We are often asked whether we believe ultraviolet illumination is necessary for snakes. Our answer typically is that while it may not be absolutely mandatory, it sure can't hurt. Water snakes seem to benefit from full-spectrum lighting, especially for basking and for their skin condition. We provide full-spectrum lighting above each cage and use color-corrected plant-growth bulbs for heating. While the amount of ultraviolet light supplied may be negligible, the color temperature of full-spectrum bulbs—a way to measure the amount of natural sunlight-like light—may be beneficial to captive snakes and is undoubtedly beneficial to insectivorous species such as rough green snakes.

Weather and behavior: Naturally changing weather patterns such as dry seasons, rainy seasons, low-pressure frontal systems, the high pressure associated with fine weather, even the lunar cycle, are known to affect snake behavior. Many nocturnal snakes are most active during the dark of the moon or during unsettled weather. Tropical snakes may be most active at the start of the rainy season or just before or just after nighttime downpours. Reproductive behavior is often stimulated by the elevated humidity and lowering barometric pressures which occur at the advent of a storm.

Water, Soaking Bowls, and Cage Humidity: Although the many aridland (desert and savanna) snake species may drink and soak less often than the more humidity-tolerant woodland species, water is important to all. Maintaining the correct humidity can be an important consideration in the successful maintenance of snakes. Species from humid areas will have shedding problems if the humidity is too low; species from desert areas can develop serious (even fatal) health problems if humidity is too high. In this latter case, aridland species such as Trans-Pecos and Baja California rat snakes may languish if kept in the perpetual high humidity of our southeastern coastal plain states. Many successful breeders of these species suggest providing water to these type of snakes only one or two days a week.

Besides serving as a drinking receptacle, the water bowl is an integral part in raising or lowering the humidity in a cage. Cage humidity will be higher in a cage with limited ventilation than in one with more.

If you wish to increase and retain a high humidity in your cage, place a large water bowl near the hottest spot. If you wish to decrease or keep humidity as low as possible, provide a small water dish and place it in the coolest spot in the cage.

Please note: If your snake is "opaque" or "blue," the condition assumed prior to skin shedding, you may want to provide a water dish large enough to allow your snake to soak. To make certain you're not depriving your animal of needed water, watch its behavior. Snakes often prowl actively when they are thirsty.

Caging

Simple "American Style"

American reptile enthusiasts usually select the bare minimum in caging. This may mean using an absorbent substrate of folded newspaper, paper towels, or aspen shavings, an "untippable" water bowl, and a hide box. Many snake species will thrive, and

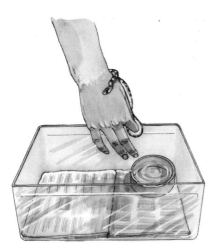

Smaller snakes may be kept in properly ventilated, plastic, shoe or sweater boxes.

A soldering iron easily melts ventilation holes (from the inside out) in plastic shoe or sweater boxes.

some (such as corn snakes and many milk snakes) will even breed in such cages.

Plastic shoe, sweater, and blanket boxes are often used, and all are available in many hardware and department stores. Be sure the lids fit securely or can be secured with tape or velcro strips. Aquariums used as terrariums are somewhat more expensive but are also readily available in pet and department stores. Locking plastic or metal-framed screen lids are standard items.

If plastic boxes are used, sufficient air (ventilation) holes must be drilled (or melted) to provide air transfer and to prevent an accumulation of humidity. We prefer ventilation on at least two sides and usually ventilate all four sides. If an aridland rat snake is being kept, we ventilate the top as well.

Cabinets that hold a dozen or more plastic boxes are now available, many with built-in heat tapes. These are advertised in most reptile magazines and are available at many of the reptile shows.

Within reason, caging snakes is a matter of individual preference. Large scale breeding facilities, such as the Gourmet Rodent, utilize large plastic sweater boxes in a rack system.

Shelving units that hold many shoe or sweater boxes are commercially available.

Glass aquaria can be oriented in either the usual horizontal or vertical position, as desired. If you use the vertical orientation, the clip-on screen

Remove the bottom of one tank and stack and seal the two to make a vertically oriented terrarium suitable for arboreal snakes.

top can serve as a side. Glue feet on the side of the tank which is underneath so that the side or top is easy to take off and put on.

Custom glass terraria can either be purchased or, if you are just the slightest bit handy, can be built. Merely take your measurements, cut the pieces of glass (or have them cut), burnish the edges, then use a latex aquarium sealant to build your custom tank. The glass can be held in place with strips of masking tape while the sealant is curing (about 24 hours). The most important thing when using the latex is to make absolutely certain that the edges of the glass that are to be sealed are entirely free of any oils or any other contaminant that could prevent the aquarium sealant from forming a tight seal. Remarkably large terraria can be held together very securely with aquarium sealant, especially if the tanks will not be used to hold water.

European Style

Unlike the plain terraria used by most American hobbyists, European hobbyists are known for more elaborate, natural terrarium interiors. The Europeans' concept of creating a miniaturized ecosystem has allowed them to breed many snake species thought difficult by Americans. The European approach matches the terrarium setting to the species.

You will have to decide which concept you prefer. It is much easier to care for large numbers of specimens in rather sterile, generic cages than in intricate terraria.

We use a combination of both concepts in our terraria. Our terraria usually have a substrate of easily replaced dried leaves for a woodland terraria or sand for a desert terraria. The water dishes are hidden behind logs gathered from the woodlands. Whenever possible, we have at least one thicket of easily grown foliage plants. We have found both Philodendron and Epipremnum (=Pothos) to be very durable in moderate light situations. Diagonal and elevated limbs are placed strategically for arboreal snakes.

Moisture content in naturalistic and seminaturalistic terraria must be evaluated frequently. If these terraria are too damp, too dry, or have incorrect lighting, the vegetation and snake inhabitants will suffer.

Feeding

Snakes exhibit all degrees of dietary generalization and specialization. There are insect eaters, worm eaters, fish eaters, and toad eaters. Many snakes feed on birds and mammals, and it is many of these snakes that are favored by American hobbyists. Rodent-feeding snakes include the boas and pythons, the king, rat, and gopher snakes, and the African house snakes.

For a captive snake to eat properly, it must be offered the correct type of food, and the snake must feel secure. An insecure snake will not feed, regardless of how hungry it may be or how tempting the prey offered.

Mechanics

Snakes find their prey primarily by sight and scent. They can, apparently, see moving objects rather well (there is some question regarding whether snakes perceive stationary objects). In addition to sight, snakes have an acute sense of smell. For example, scent molecules are carried by the tongue of the rat snake to the sensory Jacobson's organs nestled in the palate where they are then analyzed.

Snakes may overpower their prey by means of constriction, by throwing a loop of their body over and partially immobilizing a large prey item, or by eating the prey while still alive.

Constriction does not result in broken bones or any other such structural

This cage is simple and functional. To provide a thermal gradient, a heating pad can be safely secured against the bottom of the resting platform.

damage to the prey. Rather, with each exhalation by the prey animal, the constricting coils of the snake are tightened. Inhalation soon becomes impossible and the prey suffocates. Because we believe in the humane

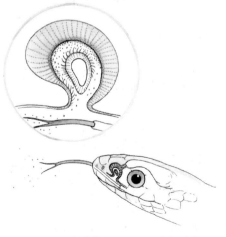

A snake's tongue brings scent particles into contact with the sensory Jacobson's organ where the scents are analyzed.

Because of the elasticity of a snake's mouth, gut, and body, comparatively large prey items can be consumed. This leopard rat snake, Elaphe situla, *is eating a white-footed mouse.*

treatment of both predators and prey, we feed pre-killed animals to all snakes that will accept them.

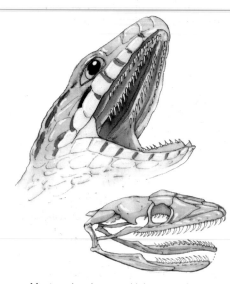

Most snakes have multiple rows of recurved teeth.

Once the snake determines the prey ready to be eaten, positioning and swallowing begins. The snake may entirely release its hold on the prey, or, while retaining its hold, sidle its jaws to the head (or, more rarely, the feet) to begin the swallowing process.

Nearly everything about a snake, beginning with the jaw structure, is "elastic." All tooth-bearing bones, both upper and lower, are capable of independent movement. Designed to retain a hold, the conical teeth are all recurved. To swallow its prey, the snake (usually) extends and then retracts the upper and lower jaw bones on one side. The same sequence then occurs with the opposite side. In this manner, a snake almost glides (or walks) around its prey. Once inside the throat, contractions of the neck push the prey into the stomach of the snake. According to ambient temperature and the metabolism of the snake, digestion may be slow or rather rapid. During this time, the snake is quieter than usual, oftentimes moving no farther than necessary to effectively thermoregulate.

Contrary to conventional wisdom, snakes neither feed entirely on live food nor do some even prefer it. We have seen snakes in the wild find and eat dead rodents. We feed our captive snakes thawed, once-frozen mice and rats.

Although most snakes are capable of eating prey items larger than their body diameter, if stressed (by fear, thirst, or temperature extremes) a snake is far more apt to regurgitate a large than a small meal. As a rule, we never feed prey items larger than the diameter of the body of the snake.

Seasonal appetites: A snake's appetite often wanes with the approach of the shorter days of winter. This is especially true if the snake is a species from a temperate area, and even more apt to happen if the snake is wild caught.

There are two things that you can do if your snake is a temperate species and a winter nonfeeder. You can either accept the situation and cool the animal into a state of dormancy (see hibernation on pages 26–27) or you can fuss with the snake, changing its lighting, warmth, and feeding parameters, and hope that you can induce feeding before the advent of spring automatically does so. Letting nature take its course with cooling is easier.

Many snakes will stop feeding during their breeding season. This period of fasting often involves both sexes and is especially seen among boas and pythons. Female snakes may experience an additional fast for several days or weeks prior to egg or clutch deposition.

If your snake stops eating (and it isn't time to hibernate or cool, it isn't breeding season, and the female snake isn't gravid), then do the following:
• ascertain that the hiding areas are still accessible
• increase the cage temperature by 3–7°F
• increase the cage humidity
• increase the daylight lighting intensity (the use of full-spectrum lighting may help offset the effects of the lessened hours of daylight)

If these methods fail, even when used in combination, try to enhance the acceptability of the prey items offered. Gory though it may seem, exposing the brain of a pre-killed food item will often induce a reluctant feeder to begin eating again.

If you've acquired a new snake and it doesn't want to feed,
• try all of the above suggestions
• try varying prey species, size, and color (some snakes might readily eat a half-grown *brown* gerbil but will refuse a brown gerbil of any other size

or a white gerbil of *any* size, or a mouse of any color—or vice versa)
• present the food *very* quietly, laying it nose first in the doorway of the snake's hidebox

Diets

Earthworms are an excellent food item for many species and subspecies of garter snakes and brown snakes. In many areas of the eastern and Pacific United States, nightcrawlers and worms emerge from their burrows after dark on dewy or rainy nights and may be collected. Worms can also be purchased from bait stores, bait suppliers (check the ads in outdoors magazines for sources), or can be raised in the cellar or garage if temperatures permit. A bed of rich, porous loam will be necessary for the worms. Although we have never been able to produce enough for our needs, raising worms does allow us to purchase a few less from bait stores.

Live feeder fish can be purchased from tropical fish stores, bait stores, or collected if laws and time allow. Many snakes will also eat frozen (and

The more terrestrial species of garter snakes (top) often prefer a diet of worms and toads, while aquatic forms, and ribbon snakes (bottom) may prefer minnows.

thawed) food fish (such as smelts) or even fish fillets. Frozen whole fish and fillets are less nourishing than live fish and often have a higher fat content. We suggest that these be used only occasionally to augment the primary diet of live fish.

Goldfish and Bait Minnows: Although goldfish are often used extensively by the keepers of fish-eating reptiles, many farm-bred fish contain an enzyme detrimental to reptile health. Goldfish should be used **only** as an emergency food source, if at all.

Frogs are a main food item of cribos, king, garter, and water snakes. There is no easy way to raise frogs for food. If it is necessary to feed these to captive snakes, the frogs must be collected from the wild. Because most frogs harbor endoparasites that may be transferred to the snakes that eat them, we suggest that you avoid using frogs as a food item. If you do feed frogs, then the snakes to which they are fed should be periodically monitored for endoparasites and purged if necessary.

Feeder frogs can be purchased in dozen or larger lots from many reptile and amphibian dealers. Some hobbyists humanely kill feeder frogs at times of the year when they are abundant for use at times when they are difficult to find.

Many species of frogs are now protected by law. As amphibian populations continue to decline, it seems likely that other species will also be protected. Some species of frogs (pickerel frogs and many tree frogs) contain noxious chemicals. It is important that if you decide to provide frogs as a food for your snakes you use only nonnoxious and unprotected forms.

Toads are the primary natural dietary item of both the eastern and southern hog-nosed snakes. All cautions regarding using frogs as a food source equally apply to toads. The introduced giant toad, *Bufo marinus*, is known to produce *very* virulent toxins.

Mice versus toads for hog-nosed snakes: See pages 15 and 96 for a discussion regarding the controversial practice of acclimating the normally toad-eating eastern and southern hog-nosed snakes to a diet of mice.

Mice and rats: Commercial breeders of mice, rats, rabbits, and chickens are a good source of feeder animals—either live or frozen (we prefer and recommend the latter because they will keep almost indefinitely in your freezer). Feeder rodents may also be purchased at many pet stores and reptile dealers or you may raise them.

Breeding mice and rats: Mice and rats are easily bred. A single male to three or four females in a 10- (mice) to 20- (rats) gallon tank (or a rodent breeding cage) will produce a steady supply of mice which can be fed to your snakes. Every 6 months, you should let some of the young grow up to replace the adult breeders and feed off the old breeders.

Aspen or pine shavings can be used as bedding for your rodents. Mice should be fed either a "lab-chow" diet that is specifically formulated for them or a healthy mixture of seeds and vegetables. Fresh water must be present at all times.

DO NOT use cedar bedding for your mice. The phenols in cedar can harm your reptiles or amphibians.

Some snakes refuse to accept lab mice or do so very reluctantly. It may be necessary for you to provide some species of wild mice (we use white-footed mice, *Peromyscus leucopus*) for problematic snake species. White-footed mice can be purchased from specialist breeders or can be collected from the wild.

Caution: Wild mice carry diseases that can be transmitted to humans. Don't handle them as casually as you might lab mice.

Live versus dead mice: We feed once-frozen, fully thawed and warmed mice to all of our snakes. In a cage, a live rodent (or even a baby chick) can become the aggressor. If, for some reason, you think you *must* feed live rodents to your snakes, then never leave the cage unmonitored while the live rodent is present.

We use several methods of thawing our frozen feeder rodents. One way is to thaw them beneath the bulbs or on the lighting reflectors on the snake cages. We also thaw them by placing them in a jar of hot water. It is *very* important that the food animals are *thoroughly* thawed before being eaten by the snake. We do *not* thaw rodents in a microwave because the thawing is not only uneven (creating pockets of intense heat while leaving other spots still frozen) but microwaving further weakens an already weakened body wall, often making the rodent entirely unusable. We often present the rodents to the snakes, nose first, in long hemostats. Most are eagerly accepted.

The (possible) benefits of a varied diet: A growing amount of evidence now suggests that what is a natural diet for a snake is the best diet in captivity. Although in the wild many snakes feed on one type of prey, other types of snakes will eat almost anything they find or kill. Humans tend to offer as food whatever is easily obtained, usually lab mice or rats. As a result, we strive to adapt toad-eating hog-nosed snakes to a diet of mice, and we feed the cribos only rats. Not enough is known about the overall effects of a mouse diet on hog-nosed snakes to make any lucid comments, and our comment regarding the indigo snake relatives is more a question than a statement. Could it be that a more natural diet would make indigo snakes, now considered one of the more difficult snakes to breed, more easily bred in captivity?

Live rodents can injure your snake. Acclimate your snake to prekilled prey.

Scenting: The technique of scenting one prey type with the odor of another is a proven way to succeed in getting *some* difficult to feed snakes to eat. This can be done in several ways. Bill Griswold, of Hogwild (Spring Hill, Florida), a specialist breeder of all three species of hog-nosed snakes, soaks mice intended as food for eastern and southern hog-nosed snakes in water in which toads have been

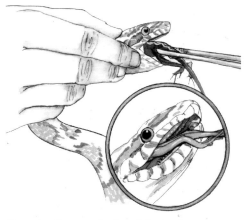

Force-feeding a snake is a delicate procedure. Some snakes will voluntarily swallow a food item if it is placed far back in its mouth. Force-feeding should be the last recourse, and even this may not always save a specimen.

Newly born or hatched snakes that refuse to eat can be force–fed with a "pinky pump."

problem. Neonate snakes that won't eat may be fed with a "pinky pump." Larger snakes may need larger meals. However, even with careful force-feeding, some snakes fail to thrive. You can do no more than your best, provided that prey of the correct size and type is being offered, that temperature and other cage conditions are optimum, and that the snake is not ill. If all of these criteria are ideal and the snake still declines, consult your veterinarian.

frozen. When one of our hatchling rat snakes is reluctant to accept a pinky, we just rub the snout of the pre-killed mouse against a live green or squirrel tree frog or touch the mouse's nose to some uric acid from an anole's stool and then reoffer the pinky to the snake. It is seldom refused.

There are times when a snake will simply refuse to feed. For these, force-feeding may be necessary, but even this does not always correct the

Health

The chances of successfully keeping a snake of any species in captivity over a long period of time is easier if you start with a healthy snake. However, determining the health of a potential purchase may be difficult to do. Snakes, like all reptiles, may show no outward signs of ill health until they are seriously ill.

Observing the basic behavior of a snake is one of the best ways to assess its condition. You should select a snake that displays an alert demeanor but is not overly aggressive, when it is disturbed. Keep in mind, however, that some species are naturally more belligerent than others and may have to be handled with a hook. Corn snakes, for example, are fairly calm, whereas a speckled kingsnake can be very defensive. Boas and pythons *normally* act very differently than kingsnakes, and a cribo or a racer is entirely unlike a rat snake in *normal* responses. Large snakes must be supported when lifted.

In addition to looking for a calm snake, choose one of the hardier species. Again, knowing that a rubber boa is a *much* more difficult species than one of the closely allied rosy boas will help you make a decision.

Select a snake that has good body weight. Although some species are normally more slender than others, a

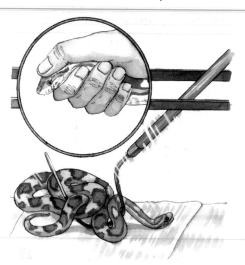

A snakehook is indispensable when moving short-tempered snakes. Gently restrain the head if the snake is in hand.

length-wise skinfold along the sides or "accordion" ribs is a caution sign. If possible, watch the snake feed.

A sneeze may indicate a respiratory infection; labored breathing may mean that lung flukes are present. Both problems are hard to diagnose in a living snake. A postmortem diagnosis is frustrating for you and pointless for the snake.

Until you are familiar with what is normal for the snake in which you are interested, it is important that you read up on the species you're interested in. This book should help, and there are several monthly publications that focus on snake behavior and husbandry. Don't hesitate to seek the advice of a knowledgeable person. Determining what is truly normal for a given species or subspecies will take hands-on experience.

If given good care, many snakes can become responsive and can live a long time. Many species live more than 10 years in captivity and some may live even to 20 or 30 years. If you choose your specimen(s) carefully, the chances are good that you will become a satisfied hobbyist.

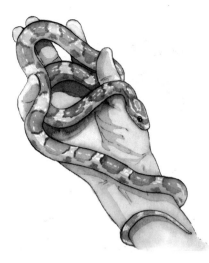
Gentle handling will quiet many snake species.

Shedding—what is normal?

The health and age of your snake will influence the frequency with which it sheds its skin. A healthy, fast-growing baby will shed its skin several times a year, much more frequently than a slowly growing adult or an ill specimen. A snake with a skin disease such as blister disease will shed frequently in an effort to rid itself of the diseased skin. If the skin problem is corrected, all evidence of the disease will often disappear after two or three sheds. Conversely, if conditions are not corrected, the problem may get worse or even fatal.

The shedding process (also called molting, or, more properly, ecdysis) results from thyroid activity. About a

Support the body of large snakes in several places. Never place a large snake on your shoulders or around your neck.

A healthy snake should have no problem shedding.

week prior to shedding, as a new skin forms under the old, your snake's pattern will dull and take on an overall grayish or silvery sheen. Its eyes will temporarily look bluish. A snake in this phase is colloquially referred to as "blue" or "opaque" by hobbyists. The eyes will clear again, and after about a week, the snake will rub its nose against a log or rough spot in its cage to loosen the old skin at the lips. Once the skin is loosened, the snake will simply crawl out of its old skin. After shedding, your specimen will again be as brightly hued and patterned as it once was.

It is important that no patches of old skin remain attached to the snake. If the snake seems to have difficulty in the shedding process, place your snake in a damp cloth bag overnight (make sure to check the temperatures). This will usually loosen the old skin and allow your snake to shed. You may have to occasionally help your snake rid itself of a particularly resistant shed.

Although in the wild snakes seldom have problems shedding, some captives may. The problem may be due to the stress experienced by a new import, dehydration, starvation, or low relative humidity in the cage.

Our tip: Examine the shed skin to ensure that the eyecaps have been shed. Sometimes the old skin may adhere to the tailtip or the eyes. If not

manually (and very carefully) removed by the keeper, the dried skin can restrict circulation, resulting in the loss of the tailtip or, if on the eyes, impaired vision and eventual blindness.

Quarantine

When you bring your new snake home, it should be quarantined for a few weeks or even a month to avoid introducing diseases and parasites to other snakes. During quarantine, observe your new snake frequently. Watch for the usual danger signs—labored breathing, sneezing, continual loose stools. Have a fecal specimen examined before you place the new specimen with those already being maintained. For this, you should seek the expertise of a qualified reptile veterinarian.

The quarantine area should be completely removed from the area in which other reptiles are kept—preferably in another room. Wash your hands between handling your quarantined and long-term specimens.

Why bother? This quarantine period is important. During this period of isolation you will be able to notice most health problems, whether established or incipient. Feeding schedules can be established, and your specimen can become at least semiaccustomed to the presence of people near its quarters. The importance of quarantine can do a great deal toward preventing later health problems.

Ectoparasites

Ticks: Snakes from the wild as well as captive specimens may harbor mites and ticks. Ticks are readily seen and removed. To remove a tick, very carefully coat it first with Vaseline or dab it with alcohol. (Use a cotton swab if you don't want to use your fingers.) After a few minutes, the tick's grip will loosen, and you can use tweezers to gently pull it out. Check that the suck-

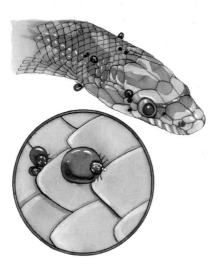

If present, ticks may be removed manually.

Place a piece of no-pest strip atop the cage to destroy mites.

ing mouthparts are removed intact, and crush it before disposing of it.

Mites: Mites are more difficult to combat because they are smaller and often present in immense numbers. A pervasive airborne insecticide such as contained in a "no-pest-strip" is an excellent combatant which alleviates the necessity of handling the snake. Remove the water dish and hang a square (about 1 inch on each side for a 10-gallon tank; 1 x 2 inches for a 20-gallon tank) in a perforated container either in the terrarium or on top of the screen lid. Your snake must not be allowed to come in contact with the strip. Leave the strip in place for 3 to 4 days, remove it (you can store it in a glass jar with a tightly fitting lid), and replace the water dish. Because the strip does not kill mite eggs, you will need to re-treat the snake and its enclosure, 9 days later, when the mite eggs have hatched. An alternate treatment is injectable Ivermectin (adminis-

tered by your veterinarian) or a dilute Ivermectin spray which you can mist onto your snake.

"Star-gazing" is one manifestation of inclusion-body disease. At the moment, this problem seems restricted to boas and pythons and can be spread by mites. Initially, the disease is difficult to diagnose and a cure is not yet known.

Burns, Bites, and Abscesses

Prevention of these problems requires just a little forethought on the part of the keeper.

Burns: Incandescent light bulbs and fixtures should be kept in a part of the cage that your snake cannot reach or cover the fixtures with a snake-proof wire cage. Make sure the surface of your hot rocks or blocks does not go above 95°F. If your snake sustains burns, cool the burned area and apply a clean, dry dressing until you take the snake to your veterinarian.

Bites: Snakes may be bitten by cagemates (usually when multiple males are housed together during the breeding season) or by feed animals. Rats being constricted may bite; a rodent left unattended in a snake's cage might chew on its predator.

Sexually mature male snakes should be caged separately and should be fed pre-killed prey. You can kill a rodent by holding its tail and then swinging it so that its head hits sharply against an edge of a counter or terrarium (we prefer to purchase frozen rodents).

Abscesses: An improperly sterilized and healed burn or bite on a rat snake may result in the formation of an abscess. Some will eventually heal and slough off or be rubbed off; a very few may require surgical removal. Consult your reptile veterinarian.

Respiratory ailments

Why it's serious: Because snakes have only one working lung, unchecked respiratory problems can become quickly fatal. The cause may be bacterial, viral, or even a parasite. A medication that works effectively for one species of snake might well not work as well for another species. Some aminoglycoside drugs ideally suited for curing a given respiratory problem may be so nephrotoxic that they can kill the snake if it is slightly dehydrated. Some bacteria are resistant to traditional antibiotics such as ampicillin, amoxicillin, tetracycline, and penicillin. We suggest that you seek veterinary assessment of any respiratory problem. You can help by quarantining the sick snake in a separate cage and by elevating the cage temperature (and sometimes by reducing the relative humidity).

Infectious Stomatitis (Mouth-rot)

Diagnosis: Uncorrected mouth rot is an insidious and common disease, that can result in permanent disfigurement and even death. Stress, mouth injuries, and unsanitary caging conditions cause this disease. It is characterized by areas of white, cheesy-looking exudate along the snake's gums. There may be enough of this material to force the lips apart. Use cotton swabs to remove the exudate. Then wash the affected areas with hydrogen peroxide. Sulfa drugs (sulfamethazine is the drug of choice) are effective against the bacteria that cause this disease. A veterinarian may suggest that an antibiotic be used as well. Complete eradication of mouth rot may take up to 2 weeks of daily treatment.

Blister Disease

Diagnosis: If your snake develops tiny raised spots or nodules (these may be hard but are often pus filled) on its skin, you should immediately assess its caging. Excessively high humidity, damp and dirty substrate, and soaking in an unclean water dish can cause this disease. Certain kingsnakes and water snakes seem especially susceptible to blister disease. Blister disease can be fatal.

To alleviate the problem, start by cleaning and sterilizing the cage. Change the substrate, put in a smaller water bowl, and remove any plants.

If the blister disease is minimal, your snake will probably enter a "rapid shed cycle" and rid itself of the problem within a shed or two. If the disease is advanced with underlying tissue damage, it will be necessary to rupture each blister and clean the area daily (for 7–14 days) with dilute Betadine and hydrogen peroxide. Again, your snake will enter a rapid shed cycle and after two sheds its skin should appear normal.

Medical treatments for endoparasites

Many reptiles, even those that are captive bred and hatched, may harbor internal parasites. Because of the difficulties in identifying endoparasites and the necessity to administer dosages based on body weight, eradication of internal parasites should be handled by a qualified reptile veterinarian. Here are a few of the recommended medications and dosages.

Amoebas and Trichomonads: Metronidazole 40–50 mg/kg orally. The treatment is repeated in 2 weeks.

Dimetridazole can also be used, but the dosage is 40–50 mg/kg administered daily for 5 days. The treatment is then repeated in 2 weeks. All treatments with both medications are administered once daily.

Coccidia: Many treatments are available.

The oral dosages of **sulfadiazine**, **sulfamerazine,** and **sulfamethazine** are identical. Administer 75 mg/kg the first day, then follow up for the next 5 days with 45 mg/kg.

Sulfadimethoxine is also effective. The initial dosage is 90 mg/kg orally to be followed on the next 5 days with 45 mg/kg orally. All dosages are administered once daily.

Trimethoprim-sulfamethoxazole may also be used. The dosage is 30 mg/kg administered once daily for 7 days.

Medical abbreviations identified:
mg = milligram
(1 mg = 0.001 gram)
kg = kilogram
(1000 grams; 2.2 pounds)
µg = microgram
(1 µg = 0.000001 gram)
IM = intramuscularly
IP = intraperitoneally
PO = orally (per os)

Cestodes (Tapeworms): Several effective treatments are available.

Bunamidine may be administered orally at a dosage of 50 mg/kg. A second treatment occurs in 2 weeks.

Niclosamide, orally, at a dosage of 150 mg/kg, is also effective. A second treatment is given in 2 weeks.

Praziquantel may be administered either orally or intramuscularly. The dosage is 5–8 mg/kg and is repeated in 2 weeks.

Trematodes (Flukes): Praziquantel at 8 mg/kg may be administered either orally or intramuscularly. The treatment is repeated in 2 weeks.

Nematodes (Roundworms): Several effective treatments are available.

Levamisole, an injectable intraperitoneal treatment, should be administered at a dosage of 10 mg/kg. The treatment is repeated in 2 weeks.

Ivermectin, injected intramuscularly in a dosage of 200 µg/kg is effective. The treatment is repeated in 2 weeks. Ivermectin can be toxic to certain species.

Thiabendazole and **Fenbendazole** have similar dosages. Both are administered orally at 50–100 mg/kg and repeated in 14 days.

Mebendazole is administered orally at a dosage of 20–25 mg/kg and repeated in 14 days.

HOW-TO:
Purchase Your Snakes from an Out-of-Area Vendor

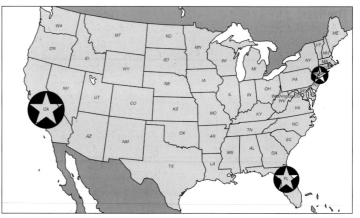

If you want to buy directly from a dealer, look towards New York, California, or Florida.

1. Determine what kind of snake you'd like to buy. Look in reptile magazines to locate dealers or breeders. Most are in New York, Florida, or California, which means you'll need to have the snake shipped to you.

2. Contact the breeder or vendor to determine the price, payment method, and shipping. Most dealers will not send animals without payment in advance, which will include shipping costs. The snake will have to be shipped by air freight.

3. Give the shipper your full name, address, and day and evening phone numbers where you can be reached. Tell the shipper which airport you'd like to use, or agree on a door-to-door delivery company. If your area is serviced by more than one airport, be very specific about the airport.

4. Agree on a shipping date and get the air bill number from the supplier. Avoid weekends when the shipping departments at smaller airports may be closed. Some shippers go to the airport only one or two days a week. Allow 24 hours for the shipping process from the shipper's airport to your airport. It may take less if there are direct flights; longer if the shipment has to be transferred from one airline to another.

5. Whenever possible, keep your shipment on one airline. With live animals, you pay for each airline involved.

6. Ship only during good weather. Your shipment may be delayed when the weather is very hot, very cold, or during holiday travel times.

7. Most airlines offer three options. The regular "space available" freight, which is the most frequently used; air express, which will give you guaranteed flights; or small package, the fastest level of service. You will pay premium rates for either of the last two levels, but they may be required by the airline depending on the weather.

8. After a reasonable time, call the airline to determine the status of your shipment. When it arrives, go to the airport to pick it up. Before you take the shipment from the cargo facility, open and inspect it before you leave the facility.

9. If there's a problem, both the shipper and airline(s) will need a discrepancy report filled out, signed, and dated by the airline.

The Name Game

As you advance in this hobby, you will definitely notice that the same snake may be called by different common names and sometimes by different scientific names. Sometimes this is honest dealer error but usually (with the common names at least) it is a part of what we call the "the name game." We find it as aggravating as you undoubtedly will. How can the name of the same species vary? And, while we're at it, of what possible good are those hard-to-pronounce Latin names?

Let's take the last first. Scientific names provide a degree of uniformity. The scientific names are always the same and are readily recognized by herpetologists and advanced herpeto-culturists throughout the world.

The art of creating or selecting a scientific name for plants and animals is called taxonomy. The method that we currently use can be credited to the 18th-century Swedish botanist Carl (Carolus) Linnaeus (von Linne). Linnaeus' first compilation of names appeared in 1735 in a publication entitled *Systema Naturae*. His method is referred to as the Linnaean system of binomial nomenclature. It essentially means that everything gets two names, much like our own two names.

The names used are based on Greek or Latin origins. For instance, a garter snake is *Thamnophis sirtalis*. *Thamnophis* is the genus (plural, genera), the equivalent of your surname. A genus consists of a group of species having similar structural characteristics. The genus is always capitalized and, if repeated usually abbreviated to the first letter (still capitalized) followed by a period.

The term *sirtalis* designates the species, a group of similar organisms that are able to interbreed and produce viable offspring. The species name is not capitalized.

Scientific names are always differentiated from surrounding text by underscoring or italicizing. Scientific names don't change, or if they do change, they change far less than common names.

Common names may vary geographically or by whim. If a snake doesn't sell well under one common name this week, a canny dealer just might change its name on next week's list. Last week's "green-lined snake" could well be next week's "emerald thread snake."

Obtaining Your Snakes

The hobby of keeping reptiles is, of course, not limited to any one region of the United States, Europe, or Asia. However, the commercial availability of reptiles is better in some regions of those countries than in others.

In the United States, for example, the major reptile dealers are in California, Florida, and New York. Reptiles are usually air freighted to pet shops and hobbyists or breeders.

We believe that breeders are one of the best sources of parasite-free, well-acclimated specimens and accurate information about these specimens. Most breeders keep records of

Open and inspect your purchases as soon after arrival as possible.

23

genetics, lineage, fecundity, health, and any quirks of the reptiles they work with. Their records are usually available to their customers.

Reptile swap meets or "expos" are another excellent source of specimens. One of the largest of these has become a two-day annual event in Orlando, Florida. About 400 breeders and dealers gather to offer the public thousands of captive-bred reptiles. At any reptile expo, we advise that you know both the product you seek *and* the vendor who sells it, either personally or by reputation.

Conservation

Conservation is no longer a concept "for the other guy." In today's world, it should be a concern of everyone, and especially for those who love nature and her creatures most of all.

Despite frequently heard arguments otherwise, it is our belief that the cause of reptile conservation is not any better served now than it was prior to the keeping and breeding of snakes became a mainstream hobby. In fact, with their immensely increased popularity, there may be proportionately more snakes being collected from the wild now than there were 25 years ago.

All indications are that many snakes, even those once thought abundant, are being seen in the wild with less frequency. We don't yet know all of the environmental pressures causing population declines, but the declines seem real. We do know that collecting from the wild for the pet and leather trades, coupled with ever increasing traffic casualties and ever fewer remaining suitable habitats, are putting pressures on native reptile populations. Each additional specimen taken out of habitat becomes proportionately more important.

We urge you to explore the joys of field study and photography as opposed to field collection of snakes.

If your budget allows, consider a photography trip to the Amazon or elsewhere with a reptile-oriented eco-touring company. We have recently taken several such trips with Green Tracks, Inc. of Tyler, Texas and Berkeley, California. On each trip we have had the opportunity to see and photograph more than 50 species of reptiles and amphibians. We believe that there is no equal to seeing snakes in their forest and desert habitats.

If collecting snakes is your goal, however, we ask that you purchase captive-bred and born specimens even if they are somewhat more expensive than wild-collected specimens.

Getting Them Yourself

Many hobbyists would like to collect from the wild a few of the snakes which interest them. One should always keep in mind that many states within the United States, most South American countries, and several European countries have strict conservation policies which require specific permits for collecting or keeping native species. We urge you to check and abide by all existing laws, both for your own area and for the area you plan to visit.

In the United States, federal laws often intermesh with, or supercede state laws. Request information from the Department of the Interior. Penalties for breach of the laws (which can apply not only to collecting, but to transportation and sale or purchase of various species as well) can be severe. John Levell has recently written *A Field Guide to Reptiles and the Law*. Laws are an always-changing process, and Levell's book includes the addresses of all pertinent protection agencies.

After checking the laws, thoroughly research the life history of the snake you are hoping to find. Many snakes are nocturnal, so be prepared to be searching at night. Familiarize yourself with all lookalike dangerous species. Above all, be very careful.

If in your field work it is necessary to roll logs or otherwise disturb the environment, alter the area as little as possible. Carefully replace all rocks, logs, fronds, or other cover after moving them. Use restraint when collecting; take only the number of specimens you need.

Transport your catch quickly and safely. Protect it from excesses of heat or cold. Small snakes may be transported in covered plastic deli cups. Larger specimens may be transported in tightly tied cloth bags.

If the collected specimens are a humidity-loving type, place a dampened, crumpled paper towel in the cup or bag with them. If desert dwellers, the paper towel should still be used, but it should be dry.

In all cases, get the snakes to their permanent cages as quickly as possible.

Breeding

Sexing your snakes: When you decide to breed your snakes, you must start with two snakes of opposite sexes. Compare the shape and length of the tail; to accommodate the hemipenes, the tail of a male is broader at the base than that of a similarly sized female. Also, the tail of the male usually tapers less abruptly and is comparatively longer. If the snake is a boid, you can compare the size of the pelvic spurs; those of the male are larger and longer than the females.

"Probing" is a more reliable way to sex subadult and adult snakes. This technique uses a lubricated probe, gently inserted into the cloaca of the snake. If the snake is a male, the probe will fit into the hemipenial pocket (see glossary, p. 106, 107), deeper than a probe inserted into a female. Learn to probe under the guidance of an experienced individual.

The pelvic spurs of a male boid are typically larger than those of a female.

If the probe used is of incorrect diameter or is forced, injury may occur.

Newly hatched snakes may usually be sexed by manually everting the hemipenes of males. This is done by placing the thumb a few scales posterior to the vent and rolling the thumb firmly, but very gently, forward. Females, of course, have no hemipenes to evert. This technique must *never* be used on a hatchling green tree python because permanent tail kinking will occur. Ask an experienced individual to guide you before you try this on your own.

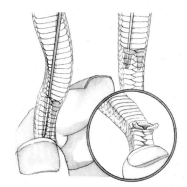

Probing is the most reliable way of sexing an adult snake (male left, female right). Hatchlings (in circle) may be manually sexed (a male with everted hemipenes is depicted) but this should be done by an experienced person (not recommended for tree boas and green tree pythons).

HOW-TO:
Winter Hibernation (not for tropical snakes)

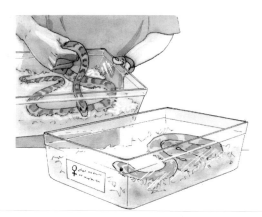

Covered plastic shoe or sweater boxes serve well as hibernating receptacles.

1. Separate the sexes.
2. Stop feeding 2 weeks prior to hibernation, and do not feed during the hibernation period.
3. Reduce relative humidity by removing items from the cage which retain moisture, such as plants and the water dish. Unless you want to use the entire cage as a hibernaculum, offer a plastic container, such as a shoe box, as the hibernation quarters.

Hibernating snakes should be provided with cool temperatures and darkness.

4. Clear a shelf in a cool, little-used closet in a basement or garage for the hibernation cage or hibernation box. Snakes need steady darkness and very cool temperatures for hibernation.
5. Hibernation temperatures should be between 48 and 56°F (9.5–13°C).
6. Hibernating specimens should be roused for a drink about every 15 days. Take the snake out of its box, place it on a shelf in front of you, and offer it water. After it drinks, place it back into its hibernation quarters. (Do not allow the snake to warm up to room temperature.) If the snake does not drink, return it to its hibernation quarters and reoffer water in a week.

7. At the end of the hibernation period, simply replace your snake in its regular caging with water dish, hiding box, limbs and plants, etc., in place.
8. Allow the snake(s) a week or so to wake up and warm up, then offer food.
9. A day after offering food, even if the snake has not eaten, put the sexes together. If courtship does not begin, mist the snakes gently, letting the mist fall like rain.

After mating, separate the snakes and offer another meal. Feed your snake(s) until they regain their prehibernation weight.

Cooling or Hibernation? Most snakes need a wintertime cooling or hibernation to trigger breeding. (Some aspects apply to all snakes; see the individual species accounts for specific data.)

In general, a snake originating from a temperate area (some rat, king, and bullsnakes; some rosy, sand, and Argentine boas among others) will require more and longer cooling than a species from a tropical area (such as boa constrictors). This is especially true for animals direct from the wild. Successive generations of captive-bred snakes do not seem to require such a precise cooling period.

Winter Preparation for Cooling

1. You'll need to separate the sexes, unless you're breeding boa constrictors. Many herpetoculturists suggest leaving boa constrictors (genus *Boa*) together at all times.
2. Stop feeding 2 weeks prior to cooling. Do not feed during the cooling period.
3. Reduce relative humidity. Cooling a room with air conditioning will drop the humidity; using a smaller water dish and removing any plants in the cage will also help.
4. Reduce photoperiod. Decrease the day length by 30 minutes each week.
5. Reduce temperature. It is often recommended that the males be cooled to slightly lower temperatures than the females. Daytime temperatures of 78–83°F and nighttime temperatures of 69–73°F are usually adequate.

After a resting period of up to 90 days, begin to prepare for spring.

Spring Preparation

1. Increase photoperiod by 30 minutes each week.
2. Increase temperature.
3. Increase relative humidity.
4. Once the snakes are alert and looking around, offer food (and once they feed, offer food again in 3 weeks or so).
5. Put the sexes together.
6. A gentle misting (simulating a rainstorm) may stimulate your snake's reproductive behavior. A simple spray bottle works fine. Aim the sprayer high so the mist falls like a gentle rain on the snakes.
7. Place a second sexually mature male in the cage. The territoriality response often turns to reproductive interest, but be prepared to intervene and remove the second specimen if necessary.

Some snakes (boids especially) are more aggressive during breeding season. This includes specimens which have never previously displayed any signs of hostility toward other snakes or their keepers. This is particularly important to remember if your snake is large. Gravid or incubating female boids of some species will become belligerent to all intruders.

As a closing comment, we wish to caution everyone with captive-bred or captive-*kept* reptiles: None should be released into the wild. Not only has it been shown that captive-produced reptiles are poor competitors, but there is the very real possibility of introducing illnesses that are potentially lethal to entire wild populations.

During the breeding season (and to a lesser degree at other times) most male boas and pythons indulge in combat to establish dominance.

HOW-TO:
Making Your Own Incubator

A homemade incubator is inexpensive to construct.

Materials

1 wafer thermostat (obtainable from feed stores; these are commonly used in incubators for chicks)

1 heat tape (available from gardening stores or hardware stores)

1 thermometer

1 styrofoam cooler—one with thick sides (a fish shipping box is ideal)

Enough ½ × 2″ mesh hardware cloth to bend into a "U" shape to form a shelf to hold the egg containers above the heat tape

Poke a hole through the lid of the styro cooler and suspend the thermostat from the inside. The L-pin "handle" on the top of the thermostat is the rheostat, and you'll use that to adjust the temperature. Add another hole through the lid for the thermometer so that you can check on the inside temperature without opening the top. If there's no flange on the thermometer to keep it from slipping through the hole in the lid, use a rubberband wound several times around the thermometer to form a flange.

Poke another hole through the lower side of the styro cooler and pull the heat tape through the hole. Arrange the tape in a continuous series of loops across the bottom of the cooler, and use wire nuts or electrician's tape to wire the heat tape to the thermostat. Put the lid on the cooler, and plug in the thermostat or heater. Wait 30 minutes and then check the temperature. Adjust the thermostat or heater until the temperature inside the incubator is about 80–86°F (27–29°C). (See the species accounts so you'll know what temperature to use.)

Once you have the temperature regulated, add your hardware cloth "shelf" and put the container of eggs on the shelf. Close the lid.

Check the temperature daily and add a little water to the incubating medium as needed. Keep the humidity high by keeping the hatching medium of peat and soil damp to the touch but dry enough so that you can't squeeze out any water when squeezed by your hand. Take care not to wet the eggs directly when remoistening the medium.

Some snakes, such as the rough-green snake, Opheodrys aestivus, *left, lay leathery-shelled eggs. Other species, such as this timber rattlesnake,* Crotalus horridus, *retain the eggs within the body of the female until the embryos are fully developed. The neonates are deposited in a transparent, membranous sac.*

Gestation and Egg Deposition

Gestating snakes need rather warm, secure areas for basking and egg deposition (or in the case of ovoviviparous species, to give birth).

The egg "box": An opaque plastic dish partially filled with barely moistened peat or sphagnum will often be accepted as a deposition site. This becomes even more desirable to the snake if it is covered, either by an opaque lid or by placing the tub in a darkened cardboard box. In both cases be sure to cut an appropriately sized access hole. If the cage temperatures are cool, the deposition tub can be set on top of a heating cable or pad (set on low) to increase warmth. Remember that heat from beneath will quickly dry the sphagnum (or other medium) and remoistening this will be necessary on a regular basis.

Female snakes investigate their cages prior to deposition, looking for the best spot to lay their eggs. Your female will probably spend some time "resting" in the egg deposition tub before she actually places the eggs there. Some snakes are a little slow to catch on; they'll spend days in the tub, but lay their eggs in the water bowl. To avoid this, remove the water dish, only replacing it for an hour or so each evening. When the eggs are

The eggs being laid by this female Plains hog-nosed snake, Heterodon nasicus nasicus, *will be gathered and incubated in a separate, temperature-controlled container.*

Baby snakes will often pop the eggs several hours prior to emerging.

laid, mark the upper surface with a penciled "X." When you move the eggs to the container which will be placed in the incubator, keep the "Xed" side up. The egg container for the incubator can be a margarine tub or plastic shoebox filled with dampened sphagnum moss. Keep the lid loosely on the container to maintain high humidity.

After egg deposition, offer the female food and step up the feedings. Female snakes that retain or quickly regain their body weight following egg deposition will breed more frequently and successfully than underweight specimens or females that are slow to recover their weight.

Incubation Procedures and Techniques

With the oviparous snakes, you need to provide correct temperatures during gestation and incubation. Incorrect incubation procedures can result in embryo deformity or death.

Incubators can be either homemade or purchased. Chick-egg incubators from any feed store are big enough for several clutches of eggs and can be used year after year.

Temperature: The suggested incubation temperature is between 76 and 82°F (24–28°C). Incubation humidity should be maintained at 80–95 percent; we keep an open container of water in the incubator. Keep the incubator dark. Once laid, eggs may be gently moved but must not be turned. Frequent handling, rough handling, and excessively brilliant lighting are not good for the developing embryos. Although most neonates have no trouble escaping from the amniotic sac, weak babies might experience troubles. This is especially true in low humidity situations where the sac rapidly dries and "toughens." If the baby seems unable to emerge from the sac, you should carefully rupture the membraneous covering.

Hatching: In nearly all cases, healthy full-term young will emerge from their eggs after about 60 days without incident. They will slit the egg with the help of an egg-tooth on their upper lip and will emerge within a day or two, peering out at intervals. In rare cases (such as when the egg membrane dries too quickly due to improper humidity), the babies may need a little help escaping. Raising the relative humidity often seems to help the most. A short slit in the top of the egg or egg-membrane may also help. Be sure not to cut blood vessels. **Caution**—if you slit an egg prematurely (sometimes only a few days) it may be fatal to the baby.

Venom

A cautionary note: Snakes of many genera, hog-nosed snakes, garter snakes, and others, possess a Duvernoy's gland. This gland, located anterior to the enlarged teeth of the upper jaw, is associated with venom production. Not all snakes with a Duvernoy's gland are considered venomous. However, in some cases, when humans have been bitten by these "harmless" snakes, reactions consistent with mild envenomation have occurred.

In reality, we know very little about the possible venomous properties of Duvernoy's glands. Toxic results have occurred from snakes as common as the backyard American garter snake of the genus *Thamnophis*. Human fatalities have actually resulted from bites by the Asian genus *Rhabdophis*. Some researchers even classify the tiny and innocuous ring-necked snakes of the genus *Diadophis* as a venomous species. In fact, new findings have led such noted researchers as Dr. Sherman Minton to pose the question "is there such a thing as a nonvenomous snake?" The answer is probably yes, but those with Duvernoy's glands should be considered at least mildly venomous.

Despite a toxic saliva, the smiling countenance of a hog-nosed snake and the fact that they seldom bite endears these snakes to hobbyists.

Some snakes, like the hog-nosed and tentacled snakes, are reluctant to bite, even when wild. Other species such as American garter and water snakes may strike and bite with even gentle handling. Always use extreme care when handling any snake.

Boas and Pythons

Boas and pythons, members of the family Boidae, are primarily tropical animals. A few of the smaller, secretive species occur in cool-to-cold temperate areas. Although some tropical species grow to immense sizes, most do not.

Boas occur in deserts, savannas, woodlands, and rainforests. They may burrow, climb, or exploit ground surface habitats; one member, the anaconda, is primarily aquatic. Except for two endangered Indian Ocean island species, all boas are live-bearers.

With but a single exception, pythons are found in the Old World. Most are ground dwellers, but most also climb agilely. One is fossorial and another is primarily arboreal. Most are excellent swimmers. All are egg layers.

Boas and pythons are comparatively primitive snakes that retain pelvic remnants that are visible as movable anal spurs. The spurs of males are usually larger than those of females, and they are used in breeding stimulation and in territorial disputes.

Pythons can make good pets, but we would like to add a word of caution: those who are thinking of acquiring one of the boa or python species that can grow beyond a handleable length of 8 feet should carefully consider their acquisition. Snakes this large can be dangerous if handled by a single individual and are difficult to place if you decide to get rid of them.

Boa Constrictor,
Boa constrictor ssp.

Mention the word "snake" to someone and the first image that comes to mind is the boa constrictor. Now scientifically designated *Boa constrictor* ssp. (the "ssp." stands for "subspecies"), these snakes were called *Constrictor constrictor* ssp. for many years.

In general, boa constrictors do very well in captivity. Freshly imported specimens may arrive with respiratory distress or mouth rot, but healthy, acclimated boas are resistant to most problems. Because the causes of both respiratories and mouth rot can vary and because cures are best determined following sensitivity tests, don't delay in getting assistance from a veterinarian.

It is only within the last decade that boas have been captive bred in any great numbers. Since then, both the normal color phases and aberrant colors and patterns have been successfully produced.

What is a "Red-Tailed" Boa? Although you can expect to pay more when buying particularly "pretty" examples of most snakes, price based on color is a fact in the boa constrictor market.

As a rule, boas from the rainforests, and especially the Amazon Basin, have tails of a deeper red than boas from the drier areas. These boas are usually referred to as "red-tailed boas" by dealers and proportionately high prices are asked for them. Most are of the subspecies *B. c. constrictor*, the Amazon Basin boa.

Common (or Colombian) Boa,
B. c. imperator

Coloration: Boas of this subspecies remain readily available. Those seen in the U.S. pet market are usually shipped from Colombia, and thus originate from the more colorful, most southerly populations of the race. They have a pleasing tan to warm brown ground color which deepens to orange or orange-red on the tail. *B. c. imperator* from Mexico and much of Central America are often of much darker ground color and heavily peppered with black. As would be expected from a race that covers such a vast north-south range, *B. c. imperator* is variable, not only in coloration, but in morphology. It has fewer than 253 ventral scales, and its dorsal scale rows, counted at midbody, number from 55–79. The dark-colored dorsal blotches from anterior nape to above the vent number 22 or more.

Size: Common boas may often attain lengths between 8 and 10 feet, but much larger sizes are documented. The largest authenticated boa of any subspecies was 18.5 feet.

Range: This race ranges southward from northern Mexico to the northern rim of the Amazon Basin.

Comments: Of the imported Colombian boas, many are now produced on "breeding farms." A greater number of common boas are now being captive bred than ever before. A common boa usually costs about $75. Unless, of course, you wish to indulge in "red-tailed" specimens (add $50) or albinos (add several thousand dollars).

At the southern end of the range we meet the **Argentine Boa** (*B. c. occidentalis*). This race, indigenous to Paraguay and Argentina, is more tolerant of cool temperatures than its congeners.

Adult Argentine boas measure a little more than 9 feet in total length. The largest females produce the largest clutches, with babies sometimes numbering in the mid-50s. Smaller clutches have been produced

Rain forest populations of the common boa, Boa constrictor constrictor, *often have a rich maroon tail color.*

by females as small as 6 feet in length.

Adults of the Argentine boa are the darkest of all of the recognized boa subspecies. At one time, there was not much interest shown in them by hobbyists. It was not until several years after the exportation of these snakes was halted (in the formative years of herpetoculture) that hobbyists

Babies of the common Colombian boa, Boa constrictor imperator, *are often offered for sale by pet stores.*

began to show a real interest in Argentine boas.

Newborn Argentines now range from $200–$350, depending on how many are actually available at any given time. Virtually all now available in the pet trade are the result of captive breeding programs.

Other Subspecies: Other popular subspecies of the boa constrictor include the **Northwest Peruvian boa** (*B. c. ortonii*); the **Bolivian boa**, (*B. c. amarali*), and the **Hog Island** (Honduras) **boa** (*B. c. imperator*).

Reproduction: In the wild, a 2 to 3 month "rest period" of cooler or drier weather is followed by increased day length, relative humidity, and rainfall. These climatic changes trigger breeding activity. Some (and preferably all) of these criteria must be duplicated in captivity if you are hoping for breeding success with your boas.

Provide fewer hours of illumination and slightly cool your boas during your winter months. Nighttime lows of 69–73°F for 6 to 12 weeks will be suitable. Daytime temperatures should range from 78 to 83°F. During this cooling period, also lower the cage humidity. Lowering humidity is most easily done by increasing ventilation within the cage (especially when your household furnace is on, which dramatically lowers available humidity) or by removing the water dish during the day. After the passing of the predetermined time, begin increasing photoperiod, warming, and raising the relative humidity in your boas' cage. This can be done gradually or at one time, as you prefer. After the boas are again active and the temperatures at their normal high, periodically mist the cage and the snakes.

Many persons prefer to keep the sexes separated except at breeding season. We have not found this to be a necessity. As a matter of fact, community breeding has proved more successful than individual projects. Heightened territorial and sexual activity can be induced by introducing a sexually adult male boa from another colony to the breeding cage. Use care when doing this; fights can ensue.

Despite our increased knowledge of their needs, the breeding of boas remains a difficult task. Captive-born specimens often breed more readily than wild ones. It may take wild-collected boas many years to acclimate sufficiently to breed in captivity. However, if you start out with immature captive-born boas, it will take them several years to attain sexual maturity.

Bred females should have suitable warmth and an adequately large hiding area. A basking area with an air temperature of 92–95°F and a substrate temperature (at the hot spot) of 94–105°F will usually be used extensively by gestating female boas of all subspecies. Improper temperatures will often result in aborted undeveloped egg masses ("slugs") or partially developed young. Even a short period of improper temperature may result in aberrantly patterned or deformed young. The fact that many of the female boas imported while gravid either abort or birth deformed babies strongly suggests that gravid females should be disturbed as little as possible.

Rainbow Boas

Brazilian Rainbow Boa, *Epicrates c. cenchria*

Although the genus *Epicrates* contains many species of West Indian boas, it is the tropical American rainbow boas that are most favored by hobbyists. Of these, the Brazilian is the most popular, followed by the Argentine and the Colombian.

At present, the importation of wild specimens of these beautiful boas has all but ceased. Because of this more limited availability, prices have climbed,

34

with, as expected, the most attractive specimens of the Brazilian rainbow boa being the most expensive.

Color and identifying characteristics: Although variably colored, the ground coloration of the Brazilian rainbow boa is brighter than that of any other. The dorsal and dorsolateral surfaces are clad in scales of rich oranges or orange-browns. Large dorsal ocelli, prominently outlined in dark brown or black, are present. These may abut or be narrowly separated from one another. The lateral surfaces are lighter and prominent black blotches, bordered above by a crescent of pink or buff (which is edged with black). The iridescent highlights from which the common name of "rainbow boa" are derived are particularly well developed in this race. Dark postorbital and midcranial stripes are nearly equally prominent. The neonates are less richly colored than the adults.

Range and habitat: This race is encountered in tropical Brazil and contiguous regions of adjacent countries. Although terrestrial (but well able to climb), these snakes may be found in river, swamp, and pond edge habitats as well as in sclerophyll woodland, thornscrub, and rainforest. Rainbow boas are often found in and near village dumping areas due to the abundance of rodent prey.

Size: The Colombian and Brazilian races often exceed a hefty 6-foot length (and sometimes exceed 8 feet), whereas the Argentine rainbow boa is of more slender build and is rarely more than 6 feet in length.

Breeding: From six to more than 20 live young are produced either annually or biennially, dependent on the fecundity of the female. The neonates are often aggressive, rather large, and will usually readily feed on small mice. Although rainbow boas begin breeding late in life, they are not particularly difficult to breed in captivity.

Reproductive behavior is stimulated in the normal manner— by first separating the sexes (optional) then reducing temperature, photoperiod, and humidity. After 6 to 8 weeks, the temperature, photoperiod, and relative humidity are again elevated, and the two sexes of boas placed together. Breeding will often quickly ensue.

Comments: The several races of rainbow boas are hardy and easily maintained, although they tend to be "snappy." The more tropical varieties can catch respiratory ailments if temperatures are low while humidity in their cages is high. In most cases, "drier is better" at cooler temperatures.

Adult rainbow boas will eat rats, mice, chicks, and small guinea pigs.

Other subspecies: The **Argentine rainbow boa,** *E. c. alvarezi,* is the southernmost subspecies of the genus. It occurs in southern Brazil, Paraguay, and Argentina. Although pretty, the Argentine rainbow boa is not as richly and contrastingly colored as the Brazilian. The ground colors of the Argentine rainbow boa are tans and buffs. It is darkest dorsally. The dorsal saddles are narrowly outlined in dark brown and the light centered lateral spots are poorly defined. Dark postorbital stripes and a less prominent midcranial stripe are present. Neonates are much more brilliantly colored than the adults.

Comments: Cooler winter temperatures are needed to breed the Argentine rainbow boa unlike its more tropical congenerics.

The **Colombian rainbow boa** is known scientifically as *E. c. maurus.* It ranges southward from Costa Rica to Colombia and may be found in contiguous areas of abutting countries as well. Adults of this race are russet to brown, and neither dorsal nor lateral blotches are much in evidence. The neonates are much more brilliantly colored and look very much like a pale

and sometimes the lips, are yellow or whitish. Color alone will identify the adults of this species. Neonate emeralds may be harder to identify because at birth they are often brick-red in color, but still with conspicuous white vertebral markings. Within a very short time an overall green suffusion becomes apparent. The emerald is the only New World tree boa species to undergo radical ontogenetic changes (those changes associated with age). Amazon Basin specimens are more intensely colored than specimens from elsewhere in the range.

Size: The emerald tree boa is, for its 6-foot (plus) length, a powerful, predatory constrictor of proportionately stocky build. Anchored securely to its supporting limb by a strong prehensile tail, the emerald boa can first strike, then drop powerful constricting coils from its leafy bower to overpower its prey of birds and small mammals.

Regurgitation: Emerald tree boas can be among the most perplexing captive snakes. If stressed in the least, many specimens develop a tendency to regurgitate their prey. The initial regurgitation may be triggered by incorrect temperatures, fright, the introduction of a new boa to the cage, shipping, an oversized meal, or several other causes. Once regurgitation has started, it can be difficult (but is seldom impossible) to stop.

Stan Chiras, a successful breeder of this species, suggests that cage temperatures for this species be kept in the 68–78°F range. Cage humidity should be high. Once regurgitation has begun, feeding attempts should be reduced to once every 2 or 3 weeks and prey size also reduced (a half-grown mouse for an adult emerald). The goal is to get the digestive system functioning again with as little stress as possible. There is a possibility that a gut stimulant may help digestion (check with your reptile

Often a brilliant orange when born, adults of the emerald tree boa, Corallus caninus *usually become a brilliant leaf green dorsally as they mature.*

version of the Brazilian rainbow boa. Like others of the genus, the Colombian rainbow boa assumes a lighter color at night.

Two Popular New World Tree Boas

Emerald Tree Boa, *Corallus caninus*
  Color and identifying characteristics: In color, adult emerald tree boas are emerald green. The only relief from the green occurs as an occasional yellow scale and a series of variable enamel-white dorsal bars. The venter,

veterinarian). If lucky, regurgitation will cease after the first try. If not, lengthen the span to the next attempt and decrease prey size even more. Using such care, Chiras has never lost an emerald.

Caging: We suggest that vertically oriented caging, replete with horizontal perches of a diameter about equal to that of the snake's body be used for this beautiful serpent. We disagree strongly with the current trend of using perches constructed of PVC, preferring instead fitted limbs with bark or grapevines. Boas are much more at ease with these naturalistic perches than with the smooth, difficult to hold PVC.

The caging used for the emeralds is similar to that described for the Amazon tree boas (see pp. 38–39).

Range and habitat: Of the neotropical tree boas, the emerald is the most persistently arboreal. Although juveniles are usually found close to the ground, adult emeralds are considered a canopy species.

Reproduction: This ovoviviparous species usually produce less than 12 proportionately large babies. Once fully acclimated, adults can be cycled by reducing winter temperature, humidity, and photoperiod. A nighttime temperature should be allowed to drop to about 70–72°F. Daytime highs can be a few degrees warmer, and a hot spot of about 82°F can be provided. Breeding will often begin with the lengthening photoperiods, increased humidity, and warming spring temperatures. Misting the specimens will provide an added incentive. Although most emerald boas will often bite with only a small provocation, breeding males can be very aggressive. It is important to use care when working with them.

Comments: Wild-collected adults can range from easy to very difficult to acclimate. Neonates are more easily acclimated.

Although emeralds were once common in the pet trade, by the early 1990s, extensive permitation procedures and seldom-granted permits restricted importation. Because of their scarcity in the pet trade, emerald tree boas are very expensive. Captive-born neonates may cost $750 or more.

Feeding: It may take considerable experimentation to induce an adult emerald to feed. It seems that emeralds are not only prey specific, but many are color specific as well. Emeralds will usually eat hamsters, white mice, brown mice, white rats, brown rats, gerbils, baby chicks, and baby quail. Neonate and juvenile emerald boas are more easily acclimated to captive diets than adults.

Emerald tree boas are easily stressed. Until fully acclimated their cage should be placed in quiet surroundings, and the snakes given ample cover. Emeralds are more of a display snake than a pet snake.

Imported specimens are often heavily parasitized. You should have a veterinarian assess the gut flora and fauna. A proliferation can cause repeated regurgitation and, if not curtailed, death.

Amazonian Tree Boa,
C. hortulana ssp.

Color and identifying characteristics: The Amazonian tree boa is the most variable of the tree boas in both coloration and pattern. Hobbyists often refer to those with darker ground colors and silvery to buff pattern components as the garden phase. Amazonian tree boas may be gray, tan, olive, yellow, orange, or orange-red ground color. Some light specimens have well-defined darker markings, some dark specimens have well-defined light markings, some may be patterned with wide bands of yellow or pale green, some may be flecked, and some may be nearly unicolored. Most specimens

The contrasting orange and brown of this Amazon tree boa may fade and meld with advancing age.

have some black or dark brown radiations near the eyes. Hobbyists eagerly seek the reddest and yellowest of these tree boas. As with many other snakes, the most attractive snakes command the highest prices.

Size: Although this species may equal or even exceed the length of the emerald boa, the lesser body bulk makes the Amazonian tree boa look considerably smaller. This tree boa can exceed 7 feet in length.

Range and habitat: The Amazonian tree boa is found over much of tropical South America. They can be particularly abundant in riveredge shrubbery, in public gardens, and in other cultivated areas. Most seem to be at home at the 4 to 15-foot level in the vegetation. Juveniles are often found very low to the ground, and occasionally adults may descend to the ground.

Breeding: Large numbers (10–20) of live young are produced by the Amazonian tree boa. The Amazonian form has been repeatedly bred by herpetoculturists. There is much interest in breeding for the reddest possible coloration.

We have seen gravid females in shipments of imported specimens throughout the summer months. Those we have bred have done so after having had temperature, humidity, and photoperiod reduced for the winter. Breeding commenced when all of these three components were increased and when gentle daily mistings were begun. Amazonian tree boas maintained outdoors in southwest Florida seemed stimulated to breed by the reduced barometric pressure that heralded the advent of a thunderstorm or frontal system.

Caging: Although an Amazonian tree boa can curl up in a remarkably small space, we suggest a vertically oriented cage of fair size. When indoors, our boas were maintained in

Red and orange specimens of the feisty Amazon tree boa, Corallus hortulana, are the most eagerly sought by hobbyists.

cages which measured 5.5 feet high and which had a floor space of 2×3 feet. The indoor cages were made of plywood and had a full-length glass front which opened for access. The cage was criss-crossed with horizontal branches. Live philodendrons and pothos served both as cover for the snakes and raised the cage humidity. When outside, the tree boas were in cages of similar size as when indoors but the outdoor cages were made of wood frames which were covered with 1/8 inch mesh-welded wire to allow unfiltered sunlight and rain to enter.

Comments: These boas tend to be snappy and adjust poorly to handling. Of the four New World tree boa species, the Amazonian race of the garden tree boa seems the hardiest at all stages of its life. Neonates will often accept small hopper mice as their first meals if teased with the morsel until they strike and constrict it. Holdouts will nearly always "break" on tree frogs or lizards, then after a few meals of these natural foods, accept fuzzy mice. Adults generally feed on laboratory mice.

Kenyan and Other Familiar Sand Boas, genus *Eryx*

Introduction: Sand boas (subfamily Erycinae) are the Old World equivalents of the New World rosy and rubber boas. The sand boas are primarily aridland snakes that often seek refuge in the burrows of small mammals and lizards. Of the 10 or more species (neither the number of species nor subspecies has ever been agreed on by authorities), only three or four are frequently seen in the European and American pet markets.

In general, sand boas are secretive snakes which are moderately flattened under normal conditions. When frightened or cold, they will laterally flatten their bodies even more to either seem more imposing to a predator or to pre-

sent more surface for thermoregulation. They tend to lash sideways to bite until you pick them up. Sand boas are specifically adapted for a fossorial existence. They have an enlarged rostral scale, heads which are not distinct from their necks, and short tails and scales which are usually smooth anteriorly but often heavily keeled posteriorly.

In the wild these snakes feed on lizards, other snakes, and small mammals. Neonates *may* occasionally eat an insect.

Kenyan Sand Boa, *Eryx colubrinus loveridgei*

Of all of the sand boa species, the East African Kenyan sand boa is most commonly seen in U.S. herpetoculture. It is no longer imported from the wild in any great numbers, and its availability is due to captive breeding.

Coloration: The Kenyan sand boa has some shades of orange, buff, or yellow dorsal and lateral markings against a brown or olive brown background color. The venter is off-white. Males tend to be more brilliantly colored than females. Albino and anerythristic strains are now being captive

The Kenyan sand boa, Eryx colubrinus loveridgei, *is now widely bred in captivity and available in many colors. This is a very brightly colored example.*

bred. The albinos are patterned yellow or cream on white; the anerythristic strain is patterned with black against a light gray-blue ground color. Although both of these morphs are in demand by hobbyists, we continue to prefer the more commonly seen (and far less costly) normal phases.

Range: Kenyan sand boas are found in Kenya and Tanzania.

Size: Adult female Kenyan sand boas are bulky and often reach 22–24 feet in length. Males are considerably smaller and of slighter build. Males may be identified by their proportionately longer and stouter tail and the larger cloacal spurs. This sand boa may deliver one or more slashing bites on provocation. However, once in hand they usually become quiet. Neonates are about 8 feet long at birth and entirely ready to bite on emergence from the amniotic sac.

Breeding: The Kenyan sand boa is an easily bred species. They require only moderate cooling to cycle reproductively. To do this, simply offer a greater daytime thermal gradient and drop the nighttime temperature a few degrees for up to 90 days during the winter months. This reduction should be coupled with a reduction in photoperiod. Our snakes are "cooled" during December, January, and February. As we always do, we continue to provide the normal, seasonally variable, hours of daylight. During this time the daytime highs do not usually rise above the low eighties and nighttime lows may drop into the mid sixties. It is not unusual for the boas to refuse most or all food during cooling. Because these snakes are normally a very robust and hardy species this seldom causes any problems. Breeding begins soon after the springtime elevation of the cage temperature.

They do well in trios (one male, two females). Young are produced annually. Parturition occurs about 4 to 5 months after breeding, in late summer or early autumn.

When our females were gravid, a heating pad (with the setting on low) was placed beneath half of the terrarium and run continuously. Except for the hottest days, when in late afternoon the summer sun would warm the entire room to the high eighties or low nineties, the females chose to have at least part of their bodies in the warmed sand atop the pad.

Clutch size may vary from 3 and 22 (usually 10 to 16) rather hefty babies. Although a few of the neonates may insist on lizards for their first meal, the vast majority will accept newly born mice. Even the lizard eaters will soon switch over to mice, especially if the pinkies are scented with lizard odor. Several of our neonates have eaten crickets that accidentally got into their cage, but we can find no reference to insects being included in the diet of wild specimens. One of the Kenyans that accepted several crickets was a neonate that had refused to eat anything we offered. After eating several crickets, the little snake ate a cricket-scented pinky mouse and then readily began accepting normal, unscented pinkies.

Caging: We found that a terrarium made from a 20-gallon "long" aquarium was ideally sized for three small boids. The substrate was of 3 to 5 inches of dry builder's sand. (Do note that sand is a very heavy medium. Be certain that your terrarium's stand can hold the weight.) A small untippable dish of clean water was presented to the boas for about 2 days once every week or two. The boas would usually investigate the dish soon after it was in place, and sometimes drink and sometimes not.

Normally, summer daytime temperatures ranging from the mid-80s to the mid-90s are ideal. A heating pad or a heat tape beneath one end of the terrarium will provide a thermal gradient.

We provide summer daytime temperatures of 92–96°F on the hot end of the terrarium. This can be allowed to cool during nighttime to as low as the mid- to low seventies.

Like other erycine species, much of the Kenyans' moisture requirements are apparently metabolized from food animals. Adult snakes are usually ravenous feeders on lab mice or rat pups.

The Rough-scaled Sand Boa, E. conicus

Next to the Kenyan sand boa, the rough-scaled sand boa is the best known and one of the calmest of the pet trade erycines.

Coloration: Against the tan, buff, gray, or yellowish ground color are three rows of large dark spots, one on each side and a particularly broad series dorsally. The dark markings may vary from reddish brown to deep rich chocolate brown to nearly black. The spots may fuse into bars or a very broad and irregular vertebral stripe. The head bears prominent postorbital stripes.

Size: Females of this very heavy-bodied sand boa may attain or even slightly exceed a 2-foot body length. Males are noticeably smaller.

Range: This savanna dweller is common to areas of India, Pakistan, Sri Lanka, and adjacent countries.

Breeding: This species seems to require considerable cooling to breed successfully. Captives can be bred annually but a biennial breeding sequence may be more normal in the wild.

This species has fairly small clutches (normally three to nine, but sometimes more) of rather large young. The neonates will usually accept pinky (or slightly larger) mice. (See also the breeding comments for the next species.)

Caging: Although rough-scaled sand boas are less persistent and

The rough-scaled sand boa, Eryx (Gongylophis) conicus, *is popular with hobbyists. Females of this Asian snake are much larger than males.*

gifted burrowers than other members of the genus, they do thrive in a "normal" sand boa setup.

The Smooth-scaled Sand Boa, E. johnii

The smooth-scaled sand boa is less commonly available than the Kenyan sand boa.

Coloration and appearance: The adults are often a dull brown coloration, but juveniles (and some adults) have varied colors. These latter have broad dark bands crossing a ground color of orange. David Sorenson, one of the premier breeders of this species in the United States, believes that pattern retention is populational at best rather than subspecific.

In gross appearance, the smooth-scaled sand boa resembles the American rubber boa. Both have a narrow head, loose skin, and a bluntly rounded tail. The smooth-scaled sand boa has a greatly enlarged rostral scale which the rubber boa lacks.

Although most specimens are brown, brightly colored examples of the smooth-scaled sand boa, Eryx johnii, *are occasionally seen. This pretty example may dull somewhat with age.*

Size: The smooth-scaled sand boa is one of the larger members of the genus, reaching or even exceeding 3 feet in length.

Range: This species is found in India, Pakistan, Bangladesh, and Iran.

Breeding: Like many other sand boas, this is a hardy and easily maintained species, but *E. johnii* very rarely attempts to bite. *E. johnii* is seldom bred successfully and seems to require a lengthy period of almost complete hibernation. Hibernation temperatures as low as 58–62°F are easily sustained by these snakes. The neonates number from two to eight and are quite large and well able to eat pinky (or slightly larger) mice. Despite its reputation for hardiness, the infrequency with which this species is bred indicates that hobbyists still need to learn more about its basic necessities.

Caging: Except when in hibernation, *E. johnii* requires temperatures near 95°F during the day but which drop by about 10°F at night. We always provide thermal gradients, with the cool end of the terrarium being room temperature (about 84°F by day and slightly cooler at night).

New World Erycines

Rosy Boas, *Lichanura trivirgata* ssp.

Introduction: In many ways, rosy boas are the perfect boa because they are small, pretty, interesting but secretive, and hardy.

Rosy boas range from central western Arizona and southern California to northwestern Mexico and over much of the Baja, to the southernmost tip. They are also found on a few islands off both Baja coasts. They frequently live in rocky hillsides, mountains, and canyons. Many of these areas have vast expanses of sandy desert which serve as barriers to prevent the wandering of these snakes from canyon to canyon.

Different populations have specific color patterns. Those from Baja have a steel gray body and narrow, precise striping (*L. t. myriolepis*). Those from Arizona have wide rust stripes on dusky gray background (*L. t. gracia*). Certain subtleties may be quite restricted. Thus, it is rather an easy matter for an experienced researcher or hobbyist to guess the origin of a given specimen. Expertise may be *so* well honed that the origin of the snake can be narrowed to a particular canyon!

We strongly urge that you retain the characteristics of the various phases and subspecies by breeding only within the same population. Most hobbyists enjoy knowing the particular canyon that their specimen is from. Intergrades and muddled morphs—"mutts" if you will—are useless and far less valuable.

Size: Rosy boas are robust. Their tail is heavy but not bluntly rounded. Adults are about 30 inches in length. They mature quickly, and at about

2 years old they produce small litters of large young.

Breeding: Rosy boas are not difficult to breed. They may be kept communally (a pair or trio) throughout the year or may be housed singly. Females may be sequentially introduced to a male's container. There are several methods of cycling all with a similar success rate.

Some breeders believe Rosy boas do best if fully hibernated for 2–3 months. Others merely allow a "substantial" cooling during which the snake receives only 8 hours of daylight.

In mid-February, the snakes are brought out of hibernation or cooling, and photoperiod is increased to that which is naturally occurring outside. After a few days of warmth, the snakes are fed a small meal.

It is important that the adults be of ample weight before breeding because males and females routinely fast. This voluntary fasting *may* last for several weeks. Males may not feed again until a week or two after the end of the breeding season. Some females may feed once or twice after having been bred, whereas other females will continue to eat throughout their gestation.

If the snakes are kept communally, they will begin breeding when ready. If they are kept separately, introduce the females to the males after several meals. During courtship, the male will zigzag himself atop the female and stimulate her with his cloacal spurs.

Gestation averages about 4 months. Females usually undergo a "prenatal shed" from several weeks to as little as one week prior to parturition. A day or so before parturition, females will usually begin restlessly prowling their cages.

An average litter consists of five to eight young which may vary in size from about 10 to slightly more than 14 inches in total length. Babies can be short tempered and very hostile at

Rosy boas vary in color geographically. Pictured are an orange and gray desert phase, Lichanura trivirgata gracia, *and a black on tan Mexican mainland specimen,* L. t. trivirgata.

even the most benign of human overtures. With growth and gentle handling, most will eventually quiet.

Habitat: Rosy boas are snakes of semiarid, rocky, and boulder-strewn habitats near desert springs, streams, and canyon seepages. They may be found from sea level to more than 4,000 feet in elevation. They wander both day and night and may be found crossing roadways in the late winter and early spring. Hot weather usually induces crepuscular and nocturnal activity or even lengthy periods of inactivity.

Two of the newer color morphs of the Burmese python, Python molurus bivittatus, *are the labyrinth, top, and the green or patternless.*

Caging: In most areas of the country, rosy boas are wonderfully hardy little snakes. In the deep (and perpetually humid) southeast, rosy boas seem sometimes to develop regurgitation syndrome. This happens especially when the high humidity is accompanied by lower than optimum temperatures. An abnormal proliferation of gut protozoans may also contribute to the problem. Regurgitation may be corrected by elevating cage temperatures to 88–92°F and by lowering relative humidity. To keep humidity low, we suggest placing the water dish in the cage for a few hours only once every 2–3 weeks. If regurgitation continues, veterinary assessment should be sought. If left untreated the snakes can weaken and die.

Rosy boas are easily handled snakes. Many rosy boas live for more than 15 years in captive life. With our increasing knowledge, we expect that the average captive lifespan will increase; other boas in this subfamily routinely exceed 25 years.

Burmese Python, *Python molurus bivittatus*

Comments and cautions: The Burmese python is the most commonly seen and often bred large python in the world. This nonendangered race of the endangered Indian python is now available in a great many colorations and patterns. It is known for its calm and placid disposition. It is important that you know that this snake will grow to be more than 10 feet in length within the first 3 years. A python this large can easily kill its human keeper, and some have done so. In most cases it is a misdirected feeding response that has led to the disaster, but regardless of the reason you can be seriously hurt.

We urge you to read the following species account carefully and to assess and reassess the wisdom of acquiring a giant constrictor. These big snakes are *not* for the casual hobbyist. There are precautions you must take that you wouldn't need with a smaller snake. It is very important that when a baby you feed your python in a box, separate from its "home" tank. This way the snake will learn to associate the feeding box, not its keeper, with the introduction of food. After handling a food animal, *before* handling your python, carefully wash the scent of the prey from your hands and arms and change clothes, if necessary. If you smell like food, your snake will treat you like food. Snakes act and react primarily on instinct, not intelligent assessment. Do not attribute to your python a power of discernment for which it is incapable.

Coloration: The normal color of the Burmese python consists of a tan to brown ground with dark-edged olive-brown dorsal and lateral blotches. A well-defined dark spearhead is present on the top of the head. Baby Burmese pythons, even when captive bred, can have edgy dispositions, but

Once selling for many thousands of dollars each, albino Burmese pythons are now hardly more expensive than those of normal coloration.

Normally colored and patterned Burmese pythons are most commonly seen in herpetoculture. When amply fed they may attain a length of more than 8 feet in the first year.

with handling and time they usually become very tame.

Variants: The first captive-hatched albino Burmese pythons were priced at thousands of dollars each. Fortunately for hobbyists, the albinos are as hardy and as fecund as their normally colored relatives. Prices for young albinos have decreased from several thousand dollars to a few hundred dollars.

Many additional "new" colors and patterns of Burmese pythons have been selectively bred and introduced. One is the **"green"** or **"patternless"** Burmese. Both names can be deceptive. The green merely means an overall olive-brown shade. As babies, most of these snakes have a reduced, but still strongly evident, pattern. The pattern does become obscured with age and may be entirely obliterated by the time the snake attains a length of 4 or 5 feet. This phase is also available in an albino coloration (the **albino green** Burmese).

A pale brown phase, called the **cinnamon** Burmese, has been developed. In the normal phase of this coloration, the basic brown tones are paler than a normal Burmese. The ground color actually nears cinnamon. Of course, both an **albino cinnamon** and a **green cinnamon** are available.

A fragmented pattern anomaly is called the **"labyrinth"** Burmese. This fragmentation has been further broken in a new morph called the **granite** phase.

As you might have guessed, in the hope of developing something new and interesting, most of the existing color and pattern anomalies have now been interbred. The result is that you often don't have the vaguest idea what colors, or combination of colors, any captive-bred pairs of Burmese will produce.

Size: An 18-inch long hatchling can reach 8 feet in length in only 1–2 years! The growth may then slow somewhat, but Burmese pythons usually reach a

The labyrinth pattern, rather recently developed in the Burmese python, is becoming a hobbyist favorite. No matter the color, be certain you can manage and house such a large species prior to purchase.

length of 12–14 feet, a housing challenge for even the most dedicated snake keeper. Sexual maturity is reached at a length of 7–10 feet. Burmese pythons are heavy bodied, and females tend to get much larger than males.

Range: In addition to Burma, Burmese pythons are found in Indonesia and Malaysia. Burmese pythons may live in a variety of habitats, ranging from open fields and farmland to woodlands and forests.

Caging: While a baby will comfortably reside in a 10-gallon tank, a 4–6 foot yearling will probably require a 55-gallon tank, and an 8-foot, 2-year-old specimen should have about a 100-gallon tank. You will probably even feel comfortable housing a 10-foot python in a 100-gallon tank. However, a 12–15-foot python will require a cage with a floor space of about 4 x 8 feet, and when the snake exceeds 15 feet, many hobbyists actually remodel and dedicate a suitably heated room to the serpents. This is

especially true if you are housing more than a single snake in the cage.

Feeding: In addition to the challenges of adequate caging, there are the challenges of *feeding* the snake. Few people object to feeding a hatchling Burmese python the required amount of adult mice, and most keepers don't even object to feeding the yearling python the number of rats it will need. Some keepers, however, are squeamish about feeding the still rapidly growing python the guinea pigs, chicks, ducks, and rabbits that it will require as a young to fully grown adult.

Breeding: In keeping with its large size, the Burmese python has large clutches of large eggs. Average-sized females often have 30–40 eggs, and very large specimens sometimes lay more than 60 eggs. Incubation temperatures of 85–88°F should be maintained, and the relative humidity should be high, but not saturated. Female Burmese pythons will readily incubate their own eggs if allowed. During maternal incubation, the female wraps around her clutch and actually elevates her body temperature to a more suitable level by initiating a series of shiver-like muscle contractions. Some females may defend their clutches, striking repeatedly as you attempt to remove the eggs for incubation, others will remain relatively benign. (See pages 28–30 for suggested incubation techniques.)

What to do with an unwanted giant snake? There are two other problems you need to consider. Many keepers of Burmese pythons decide when their snakes reach 7–8 feet that these snakes *really are* too big. A 7–8-foot Burmese python is difficult to get rid of. Other hobbyists don't want it; zoos and nature centers usually already have their own specimens or aren't interested in dealing with a snake that large. Breeders will sometimes buy or take a large python back, but medium- to large-sized Burmese pythons can be *very* difficult to place. You should consider this problem before you acquire that cute little baby.

Laws: Burmese and other large pythons and boas may be illegal in some communities. This is especially true when they reach sizes of 6 feet or more. Check your local and state laws.

More Comments and Cautions: In the mid-1970s, breeders of snakes finally realized that a yet unplumbed market truly existed for Burmese pythons. The race was not endangered, importation was only partially regulated, and availability was rather uncertain. The breeders hypothesized, rightly it turned out, that if baby Burmese pythons were offered at a reasonable price, sales would increase exponentially. It would then become worth the effort to set up breeding colonies of these snakes. As a result, commercial and home breeders of Burmese pythons sprang up across the world. The result was that thousands of baby Burmese pythons were ready for the pet market—and at about the same time albino Burmese pythons became available. The combination of the two—normal-colored babies which sold for reasonable prices and albino babies which brought sky-high prices—took sales of Burmese pythons to dizzying heights!

The reticulated python, *Python recticulatus*, is a big, often bad-tempered, python native to Asia but which is now captive-bred in large numbers. We do not recommend it as a pet because of its habit of determined slashing, biting, and untrustworthiness.

Ball Python, *P. regius*

When frightened, the ball python has the habit of rolling into a tight ball with its head hidden near the center of the protecting body coils. This attrac-

Although reticulated pythons are considered suitable only for very advanced hobbyists, interesting patterns are now being developed by breeders. This striped phase "retic" was produced by Al Baldogo. It is also called the super tiger phase by hobbyists.

tive short python is one of the most commonly seen species in the American pet trade. It makes a calm, easy-going pet.

Coloration: Ball pythons are normally available in an attractive black and tan coloration. Other colors are also available, including **golden**, axanthic (lacking yellow), striped, a yellow and brown **"jungle" phase**, and **piebald** and **albino** phases. Unlike the normal phase imports which may sell for less than $50 each, these special color phases may cost several thousand dollars each! Before you buy one of these unusually colored ball pythons, be aware that, in at least some cases, unusual colors may be temperature-derived oddities caused by high incubation temperatures.

Behavior: Although more terrestrial than most pythons, the ball python will occasionally climb to considerable heights. This is an adaptable species in the wild. It is found in scrub, semiarid-land and agricultural habitats. When hunting, ball pythons frequently follow rodents and other small mammals far back into their burrows.

Appearance: The head of the ball python is broad and distinct from the neck. Heat-sensitive labial (lip) pits are present. This is a small but heavy bodied snake. It is known to attain a maximum length of about 6 feet, though most adults are between 3.5 and 4.5 feet. Even at this smaller size they are of impressive girth.

Availability: Ball pythons are one of the more "readily available" and inexpensive python species offered in the U.S. pet trade. Ball pythons were once as readily available in most European countries as in America, but the sales of wild-collected snakes has been mainly curtailed throughout much of Europe.

Origin: Most ball pythons in pet markets are from tropical western Africa. Unfortunately, 99% of these snakes are either straight from the wild or are captive hatched from eggs laid by wild-collected females. Upwards of 40,000 (and probably close to double that number) ball pythons are imported annually for the American pet trade.

Feeding: Pet market hype accounts for much of the ball python's popularity. Ball pythons are frequently described as the "ultimate" pet snake. In some cases, such as when hatchlings that feed on domestic mice are sold, this *might* be a fairly accurate statement. However, when wild-collected half-grown or adult specimens are sold, the story changes.

Typically, ball pythons stop feeding during the winter (their dry season). Reproductively active adults may also stop feeding during the breeding season. Female ball pythons usually refuse food when gestating and incubating. Long-term captives, including captive-hatched examples, may fast during these periods.

In addition to their seasonal fasts, ball pythons are noted for "prey imprinting." That is, they want only the particular kind of prey animal they fed on in the wild. This may be a gerbil or an obscure rodent species not available here. Such snakes may hold out until nearly starved before accepting a commercially available rodent.

If you have a wild-collected ball python that refuses to eat, you may be battling a dietary preference or a normal feeding cessation. For these reasons, we strongly urge you to avoid this sort of frustration by purchasing only a ball python—hatchling or adult—you have seen feed.

Hobbyists seem especially fond of ball pythons, Python regius, *with aberrant striped, top, or a large amount of gold, bottom, in the pattern.*

If you are having a problem getting your ball python to eat, however, experiment with all types and colors of available food species—try gerbils, mice, small rats, and hamsters; try various colors; try all both alive and pre-killed. When you attempt the live prey, introduce the prey alive (*do not* leave the live prey unattended) in the early evening. When you try dead prey, first warm it (not in a microwave oven!) to normal body temperature, then place it in the door of your snake's hide box. Sometimes exposing the brain of a pre-killed animal will induce your snake to eat.

After trying each of these methods and still finding that your ball python refuses to accept food, you will probably be ready to agree that ball pythons just might *not* be the fail-safe pet species that they are said to be! You'll concur even more with that assessment if it finally becomes necessary to force feed your specimen to save it from its self-imposed fast (see pages 15–16 for information on force-feeding). Do not rush to this action, however. Ball pythons are capable of maintaining extended fasts with no permanent impairment. Some specimens have refused to eat for a year or more before breaking their fast. A fast of this duration may actually be more taxing on the snake's owner than on the snake.

Longevity: Despite the dietary problems that prevail with many freshly imported specimens, acclimated ball pythons can be hardy, easily kept, and long-lived snakes. Longevity records note a captive life of 20–47 years!

Caging: Because they are quite inactive, even adult ball pythons may be kept in relatively small cages. A cage with a floor space of 18 × 36 inches is large for a single adult snake or for even a pair of average-sized snakes.

Despite being heavy bodied, ball pythons can climb adeptly. We therefore provide a minimum cage height of 2 feet and elevated perches. We also provide two hide boxes in each cage—one positioned over and warmed by a heating pad and the other at the cool end of the cage. During cooler weather, most ball pythons preferentially choose the heated hide (this is especially true of gravid females), but may thermoregulate by moving with some degree of frequency from one to the other.

Breeding and Sexing: Acclimated ball pythons are not very difficult to breed. Like all short-tailed python species, however, they **can** be tough to sex properly. Probing seems to be the most definitive method but even this can be inconclusive sometimes.

Cycling your ball pythons for breeding is accomplished in the same manner as with other pythons and boas. The snakes should be well fed and heavy bodied, but not fat. Adequate body weight is important because sexually active (or receptive) ball pythons may decline food, often for many weeks.

Begin the breeding sequence by separating the sexes and reducing the winter cage temperature, photoperiod, and relative humidity. During the cooling period, a daytime high of 76–80°F and a nighttime low of 68–70°F will suffice.

After 6–8 weeks, elevate all of the climatic factors to their normal summer levels and place the sexes back together. With luck, breeding will soon begin. To stimulate breeding activity even further you may temporarily place a second sexually mature male specimen with the pair. Territorial defense will usually ensue, often changing to a breeding response along the way. An occasional gentle misting, especially during barometric changes, may also provide desired stimulation.

Although it often attains an adult size of 9 to 11 feet, the coastal carpet python, Morelia spilota mcdowelli, *is a popular snake because it is the least expensive race.*

At the time, wild-collected carpet pythons sold for $15–$20 each, and the diamond pythons for $30–$40.

Then, carpet and diamond pythons were suddenly no longer available in the United States. A few were present in zoological collections, an additional few remained in private collections. It is from these few snakes, along with occasional imports from European hobbyists, that today's ready availability has evolved.

Captive breeding of these snakes does have a disadvantage. Hobbyists can easily bring together snakes from widely disparate geographical origins. When these snakes are bred, however, you no longer have a snake from northern Australia or a snake from a tiny valley in eastern Australia. Instead, you have a batch of intergrades. We strongly urge hobbyists to retain the integrity of the many phases of carpet python. It is only by breeding the various phases in the purest possible form that we will preserve the diversity of color now associated with this snake.

Ball pythons lay small clutches (one to nine, usually three to six) of large eggs. At a temperature of 88–92°F (with a relative humidity of 82–95 percent) incubation will last for about 2 months.

With time, captive-breeding programs will provide us with an increasing number of domestically raised specimens. This will lessen the pressures of the pet industry to obtain wild-collected specimens.

In addition, as more are produced, the price of aberrant specimens will diminish somewhat. However, because ball pythons have very small clutches, it may be many years before some of the most unusual variants drop sufficiently in price to become regular pet-market items.

Carpet Pythons, *Morelia spilota* ssp.

Before the early 1970s when Australia began to prohibit exportation of native wildlife, the carpet and the diamond pythons were commonly seen in the United States pet trade.

Coastal Carpet Python (*M. s. mcdowelli*)

This subspecies is the most commonly seen carpet python in U.S. herpetoculture and the largest of the carpet pythons. It is large, robust, vigorous, and hardy. Although the adults of many populations seldom exceed 7 feet, those of others regularly grow to more than 10 feet. Most carpet pythons seem to "bulk up" earlier in life than the allied diamond python, thus a healthy specimen of 10 feet or more is a truly impressive snake.

Coloration: Although varied in coloration, most coastal carpet pythons are comparatively dull. The ground color may be yellow, cream, tan, or light-to-dark brown, over which are bands, spots, or stripes of darker brown or black. On some specimens the dark color predominates; on other specimens the reverse is true.

Range: The coastal carpet python ranges throughout most of the Cape York Peninsula, Queensland, southward to northern New South Wales.

Other subspecies: Although several other subspecies of carpet pythons are recognized, all but the beautiful **"jungle" carpet python**, (*M. s. cheynei*) of northeastern Australia are uncommon in U.S. herpetoculture. This is the most attractive of the carpet pythons, and the favorite of most U.S. herpetoculturists.

The color variability that we mentioned earlier pertains to the jungle carpet as much as the other races. Jungle carpets can vary from rather precisely delineated bands of bright yellow and black to an olive-tan ground color with broad, darker edged brown bands. Other phases include irregular but bright yellow bands against a black or brown ground, a pattern of yellow or cream bands or spots against a ground of black, and a series of light dorsal blotches or saddles either above or alternating with light lateral blotches. The light blotches of this latter may be regular or irregular and may be a rather bright yellow, but are usually cream to tan. Striped specimens have occasionally been found. In most cases the stripes are better defined anteriorly than posteriorly. In addition to the stripes, the more typical blotches may, or may not, be present. Dark ocular stripes are always prominent. We had two large males that darkened with every shed until they were nearly monochromatic black. As you now know, the mere acquisition of a Tableland carpet does not necessarily assure that you will have one of the coveted yellow and black specimens. In most cases (but not always), brilliantly colored parents beget brilliantly colored progeny. Thus, knowing the color of the parent specimens will help

The jungle carpet python, Morelia spilota cheynei, *is the most brightly colored of the several subspecies.*

you make an informed decision. If you are able to acquire a 1–2-year-old carpet python (when color changes have at least begun and patterns are well developed), you will have an even better idea of what it will look like as an adult.

Although hatchlings may bite persistently, adults of the jungle carpet python are usually easily handled.

51

The clutch size of the jungle carpet python varies considerably. The average is about 15 eggs, and the largest recorded number was 28. The largest number produced by females at the Reptilian Breeding and Research Institute was 22.

The adult size of the Atherton Tableland carpet pythons is usually 6–8 feet.

The **northwestern carpet python** (*variegatus*) ranges eastward in coastal areas from the southwestern Cape York Peninsula to northern western Australia. This is apparently also the subspecies which is found in New Guinea. This is an attractively patterned python with strongly contrasting, darker edged, irregular bands of brown, black, or red on a straw yellow ground. Hatchlings are usually reddish but become less so with age. This race attains a length of about 6 feet. It is now readily available in U.S. herpetoculture.

Of the various carpet python subspecies, the yellow-specked black nominate form of forested eastern New South Wales is the most difficult to obtain. This is the beautiful **diamond python** (*M.s. spilota*). We have also found it to be the most delicate of the several subspecies. Diamonds attain an adult length of nearly 7 feet.

Intergrades: Several races of the carpet python have now been interbred with the diamond python. Such crosses are well established in U.S. herpetoculture. These intergrades are beautiful snakes with immensely variable patterns and colors. Most look far more like their carpet than their diamond parent. Displaying what we often term "hybrid vigor," these intergrades are usually eager eaters and are often very easy to breed. Although it may not be necessary, we recommend the slight dropping of winter temperatures (70–72°F night low, 78–82°F day high), a slight reduction in relative humidity, *and* the reduction of photoperiod.

Like the diamond and carpet pythons, the intergrade snakes breed in the winter, lay their eggs in early spring, and the 15 to 26 eggs hatch in late spring and early summer. The hatchlings are large and robust and readily accept rodents as their prey.

Breeding: In all of its many phases, forms, or morphs, the carpet python is both hardy and breeds readily with only a moderate winter cooling (especially carpet pythons from more tropical areas). Reduced photoperiod during the period of cooling is also important. Innumerable breeding successes have now made even the once seldom seen Atherton Tableland morphs readily available to those who want them. Prices range from about $100 for coastal Queensland carpet pythons of average appearance to $300 for the attractively colored Atherton Tableland phases. The coveted diamond–carpet python intergrades cost about $300.

The size, age, and health of the females and the subspecies involved determine the clutch size. We have

In American herpetoculture, the beautiful diamond python, Morelia spilota spilota, *remains a seldom seen and very expensive subspecies of the carpet python complex.*

had as few as 10 eggs from a small, young jungle carpet to more than 30 eggs from a large coastal carpet python.

As with most pythons, there are several ways to enhance your chances of breeding success with carpet pythons. The first way is to properly cycle your snakes. A winter regimen that will be perfectly fine for a tropical carpet python may not suffice for a carpet python that has originated from the more temperate southern extremes of the continent or for the diamond python. For more tropical pythons, a cooling during November and December to nighttime lows of 70–72°F and daytime highs of 78–82°F will suffice. It is either following or during their period of cooling that carpet pythons will usually begin their breeding sequences.

Except during periods of low barometric pressure (when they are sexually active at all times of day), most breeding activity by carpet pythons seems to occur in the late afternoon or early evening. Once stimulated, breeding activities, including copulation, may continue throughout the night and well into the next day. Although, if properly cycled, carpet pythons seldom need additional stimulation during periods of low barometric pressure (such as during the passage of a frontal system or at the advent of a severe thunderstorm). Gently misting the snakes may make them even more ardent. The misting can also be effective at other times. During stable weather, gently misting the cage once or twice in the late afternoon or early evening may activate your snakes.

The introduction of a new female or a second male to the cage of a cycled male may also provide breeding incentive. Do be advised, however, that the meeting of a second male carpet python by a sexually active snake can result in combat that can have devastating results (diamond pythons seem to not show overt aggression). Except for the breeding season, male snakes of all races may be either benign or only moderately agonistic toward each other. Supervise your specimens at all times and be ready to remove the nondominant male immediately if necessary. In many cases, the stimulation created when the second male is introduced will be immediate and will continue even after his removal. In addition, it is now known that introducing the recently shed skin of another male is nearly as effective a way to provide breeding stimulation, and it has none of the "worst-case possibilities."

Be particularly careful when handling (introducing, moving, removing) your male snakes at this time. Normally tractable snakes can become fully adversarial in only a moment.

The eggs of all of the subspecies of *M. spilota* are easily incubated, and the hatch ratio is usually excellent. One hundred percent hatches are not uncommon. Incubation temperatures between 88 and 92°F seem best. High relative humidity should be maintained in the incubator. Although hatching usually occurs after about 2 months of incubation, eggs incubated at the higher temperatures hatch in less time than those maintained at lower temperatures. Embryo deformities and fatality may occur if eggs are incubated at temperatures above 92°F. For this reason, in relatively unsophisticated, homestyle incubators which are subject to 2 or 3°F variations. We suggest a lower than maximum incubation temperature.

Behavior: Wild-collected specimens can be short tempered and untrustworthy, but will usually tame if handled gently and persistently. Once past the "snappy" hatchling stage (when all snakes are often prone to biting both the hand that handles and the hand that feeds), most captive bred carpet pythons are remarkably placid.

Caging: Despite their moderate to large adult size, diamond and carpet pythons are quite arboreal. This should be taken into account when providing housing for the snakes.

Carpet pythons are both hardy and attractive. They may be considered an excellent choice for either novice or advanced keepers.

Green Tree Python, sp.
Morelia (Chondropython) viridis

Coloration: Although dull to bright green is the most common base color of adult green tree pythons (often referred to as "chondros" by hobbyists, a reference to an outmoded scientific name, *Chondropython viridis*), blue or yellow specimens are occasionally seen. An irregular and variable white vertebral stripe (or spots) is usually present. Blue markings are also often present on dorsal or lateral surfaces. Specimens originating from Aru Island are of a deeper green dorsal coloration and have powder-blue lips and venter.

Although yellow is the most common color of hatchling green tree pythons, Morelia (Chondropython) viridis, burgundy and orange are also seen.

Hatchlings are remarkably variable. Although most are brilliant yellow with a brown middorsal stripe and irregular brown flecking on the sides, some may be brick-red, russet, or chocolate brown. The brilliant juvenile coloration is soon replaced by the green of adulthood.

Size: Although occasionally attaining a 7-foot length, most adult green tree pythons are 6 feet. Neonates are about 1 foot when emerging from the egg.

Range: This attractive python occurs widely in suitable habitats over much of New Guinea. It is also found on the Cape York Peninsula of northeastern Australia. Although far from helpless on the ground, green tree pythons are primarily arboreal. They are often seen coiled amid or atop clumps of epiphytic plants or lying quietly coiled while draped over a branch.

Breeding: Green tree pythons are an oviparous species. About 1 month after being successfully bred, ovulation occurs. It is about 1 to 15 months later that the female chondro lays her clutch of 10–25 eggs. Females incubate and protect their eggs. Incubation for fertile eggs usually lasts 56–63 days. A single clutch of eggs can produce hatchlings of several different colors, as mentioned earlier.

Although chondros have been bred by hobbyists for many years, they have remained one of the more problematic species. Egg death of the young after full-term development is common. Many hypotheses for this have been broached, but Trooper Walsh of the National Zoo, believes that it is most likely due to a failure to reduce temperatures slightly during the final week of incubation. After years of monitoring the temperatures of maternally incubated eggs, Walsh has found that female chondros allow such a temperature fluctuation, with the first and final weeks being the cooler. Walsh especially stresses the importance of cooling the clutch on the tag end of the incubation period. A temperature regimen with which he has been most successful is as follows: first week, 83°F (29.5°C); final week, 82°F (29.0°C); interim weeks, 89°F (32.0°C) days, with a slight drop to 86°F (30.5°C) nights. The relative humidity must always be "high" (95 percent or more), and good ventilation is a necessity. With this regimen, Walsh has established a 90 percent and better hatch rate.

Secure arboreal situations are chosen for the deposition site. In the wild this site may be amid epiphytes or in a broad, secure crotch. In captivity cockateil nesting boxes or an elevated wooden or plastic platform are accepted. As in the wild, a captive female will incubate her clutch if allowed. Incubation usually lasts less than 2 months.

Caging: Height and secure perches are more important to the well-being of green tree pythons than floor space. Tree limbs and a hide box affixed at or near the top of the cage offer the snakes the feeling of security that they need. Until fully acclimated, some chondros do not recognize a bowl as a drinking water source. They will, however, drink droplets of water from their coils if they are gently misted. Our breeders, kept outdoors for much of the year, were most active during the atmospheric pressure drops that were associated with our frequent thunderstorms. At that time they would feed, prowl, drink, and defecate. Misting the snakes from above with a hose would also activate them, but not to the extent of a natural storm. Interestingly, many herpetoculturists believe that the low pressures typically associated with storm systems stimulate chondros to breed, even when they are in indoor cages.

Adult green tree pythons are normally a bright green, but hobbyists are striving to develop yellow and blue strains.

Comments: This beautiful snake is still often referred to by its older name of *C. viridis*. Like many arboreal snakes, chondros are laterally compressed and have a strongly prehensile tail. They are wait-and-ambush feeders and often constrict their prey while hanging from a branch, supported solely by their tail. Small rodents, lizards, and frogs are accepted by the hatchlings. Adults seem to prefer suitably sized mammals and birds, but will accept lizards as well. Because their "prey-capture instinct" is stimulated by movement, hatchling chondros often ignore quiescent "pinky" mice. The little snakes are

The Australian spotted python, Antaresia maculosa, *is becoming quite popular with hobbyists around the world. It is one of the smallest python species.*

python. (Children's pythons *per se* are very rarely available in pet stores due to their high cost.)

Coloration: This interesting little constrictor has a ground color of variable olive against which the very irregular brownish to reddish-brown dorsal and lateral blotches contrast strongly.

Size: This species reaches a rather slender 3 feet.

Range and habitat: This is a woodland, forest, and semiaridland species of eastern and northeastern Australia.

Breeding: The spotted python is an easily bred small python that lays clutches of from 2–12 fairly large eggs. They usually require only a slight reduction of winter temperature concurrent with a lowered humidity to cycle. The eggs are easily incubated, hatching about 2 months after deposition (when incubated at 85–90°F). The hatchlings usually feed readily on pinky mice.

The spotted python is a remarkably calm, hardy, and temperature tolerant small python. Its diminutive size allows a pair or a trio to be kept in a 30-gallon terrarium. They feed readily on mice and newly born rats.

much more apt to accept older mice ("jumpers") that are moving quickly about.

Although we have always considered chondros a "just look, don't touch" kind of snake, others may enjoy handling their snakes. Green tree pythons vary tremendously in temperament. Some are defensive and irascible, whereas others are relatively quiet and approachable. Most are somewhere between these two extremes, being approachable at times but striking and biting at other times. It is usually possible to handle safely even the worst-tempered green tree python by manipulating it gently with a snake hook. From the hook the snake can be placed on a limb or other inanimate perch where it will coil and often stay (unless moved again) for long periods of time.

Spotted Python, *Antaresia (Liasis) maculosus*

Until recently, this little python was considered merely a dark Children's

West African Burrowing Python, *Calabaria reinhardtii*

Coloration: The ground color of the burrowing python is deep reddish-brown to bluish-black. Irregular patches of orangish to pinkish spots and blotches are present. Opalescent highlights are obvious. When entering the shed cycle, burrowing pythons become a translucent silvery-black.

The blunt, club-shaped tail is dark (often black) with conspicuous white subcaudal blotches. When the snake is balled up in a defensive posture, its tail is usually well in evidence, often protruding boldly outward from the tight coil of the body. This posture is a common protective ploy for blunt-tailed snakes of several families. The supposition is that an antagonist would then worry about the exposed tail and ignore the hidden head. Despite their shyness, they never bite.

The burrowing python has a gently rounded, enlarged rostral scale and a supple, well-muscled, cylindrical body shape. The head is not distinct from the neck. The scales are smooth. The eyes are comparatively small, somewhat protuberant, and have an elliptical pupil.

The burrowing python is the only truly fossorial member of the subfamily Pythoninae. When frightened, the burrowing python forms a ball with its head drawn tightly downward against the neck and hidden in the coils.

Range: Forested areas of tropical West Africa.

Food: Some burrowing pythons will accept suitably sized lab mice, but many prefer newly born rats.

Caging: Because it is a small, quiet, and secretive species, burrowing pythons do not require large cages. We keep our burrowing pythons in a 20-gallon terraria with a substrate consisting of several inches of barely moistened, loamy soil over which is a layer of fallen leaves 1–2 inches thick. These snakes are well adapted to dig burrows of their own but are also able to utilize the burrows of small rodents. As often as not, our burrowing pythons are found lying beneath the leaves, but atop the soil, in their terrarium. A small, untippable water bowl should be present, and the humidity in the terrarium should be kept high but not saturated.

Breeding: Captive burrowing pythons have proved difficult to cycle reproductively. Although some hobbyists suggest that a period of cooling and fasting is required to effect the reproductive cycling of burrowing pythons, this seems unlikely. Others hobbyists suggest that the reproductive cycling of *Calabaria* is induced by varying humidity and substrate moisture levels. Considering the tropical forest humus habitat of this snake, it seems likely that the latter would be the *major* determinant. However, when moisture and humidity levels are reduced (even in tropical forests, as during a naturally occurring dry season), temperatures often do drop somewhat. Although this natural reduction of temperature and humidity may not induce a cessation of feeding by the inhabitants, the creatures *may* feed somewhat less often. We do suggest that captive *Calabaria* be fed throughout the year, including during their gestation period.

Hobbyists may eventually find that a combination of *slight* cooling and reduced humidity for 30–45 days, followed by warming and increased humidity might cycle *Calabaria* more reliably than either method alone. Humidity can be elevated and retained by frequent gentle mistings of the substrate surface with tepid water.

Female burrowing pythons lay from one to five (often three) large, elongated eggs. The hatchlings vary from

Although very secretive, the little West African burrowing python, Calabaria reinhardtii, *is now regularly seen in the American pet trade.*

10–12 inches in length. The hatchlings are far less retiring than the wild adults and are kept in a utilitarian terrarium, with only newspaper for a substrate. In such a habitat the little snakes thrive, accepting mice from your fingers. A burrowing medium is not necessary (but a high humidity is).

Eggs incubated at temperatures between 87 and 90°F have hatched in approximately 50 days. A baby which hatched after 88 days from an egg incubated at "room temperature" (about 81–84°F) was undersized and had spinal kinks. It was euthanized, and an incubator was employed for eggs which followed. Incubator babies have averaged slightly more than 12 inches in total length. Hatchlings seem to show little balling (defensive) reaction when gently handled.

Comments: As with any snakes that are wild collected and imported as adults, it has been difficult to determine the life expectancy of *Calabaria*. Wild specimens, age unknown, have lived for more than 6 years and some to about 10 years as captives. Now that we have captive-hatched babies to monitor, it seems likely that we will find that *Calabaria* are not only hardy, but at least as long lived as some of the smaller erycine boas. We have found that if cage temperatures drop too near or below the mid seventies, *Calabaria* are apt to regurgitate their meals. The larger the meal fed when temperatures are cool, the more likely the snake is to regurgitate. Thus, even here in Florida, we now keep an undertank heating unit in place beneath one end of the terrarium. In all but the very warmest weather, we provide a thermal gradient for the snakes. The hot end of the terrarium is retained at between 87 and 90°F, whereas the cool end is usually at ambient room temperature, but never below 78°F.

Because most burrowing pythons now available in the pet trade are wild-collected imports, you should check them for endoparasites as soon as you receive them. You should be ready to experiment with prey acceptability. However, other keepers have found (as we did) that imported adults may insist on pinky rats—at least initially.

Arnold Kluge (1993) has suggested that both the burrowing python and the rosy boa (*Lichanura*) are congeneric with the rubber boa (*Charina*) and should be placed in this latter genus. This proposal has met with immense resistance from conventional taxonomists and, at the moment, general acceptance seems unlikely.

Colubrine Snakes

We now enter the realm of the colubrine snakes (family Colubridae). This vast family contains more than 1,500 species which are, collectively, referred to as "harmless snakes." This is somewhat of a misnomer, for among the colubrines are many species with enlarged teeth at the rear of the upper jaw and venoms of varying toxicity. Other species with no enlarged teeth may have toxic saliva.

We discuss none of the truly rear-fanged snakes in this section, but we do mention the hog-nosed snakes (members of the subfamily Xenodontinae), which are perpetual hobbyist favorites with enlarged teeth and a questionable toxicity. The rat, king, gopher, indigo, house, and green snakes are members of the subfamily Colubrinae. The garter and water snakes and their allies are members of the subfamily Natricinae. Variable adverse reactions have occurred from bites from members of this latter family.

The colubrines employ numerous feeding strategies. The rat, king, gopher, and house snakes either trail or ambush their prey, which is then killed by constriction. Indigos swallow their prey alive, often immobilizing large prey items by throwing a loose coil over and pinning it to the ground. Garter, water, brown, and green snakes eat their worm, fish, slug, and insect prey alive. Hog-nosed snakes can be messy eaters, puncturing and bloodying inflated toads with their long rear teeth.

The dispositions and handleability of colubrines varies both by species and by individual. Although American corn and rat snakes and European rat snakes may bite, they usually rapidly become tractable if gently handled. Asiatic rat snakes may be persistently feisty. Frightened garter snakes may bite and smear musk or feces when restrained. Kingsnakes may coil quietly around a hand or arm, and then seize and chew that hand animatedly. Milksnakes tend to be squirmy, to occasionally bite, and may never become entirely at ease when being handled. African house snakes are usually relatively placid. Until they are used to handling, the tropical indigo snakes may strike and bite savagely. If frightened, hog-nosed snakes hood, writhe, and if additionally stressed, roll upside down and play dead. Green snakes may writhe and gape, but almost never bite or smear cloacal contents.

The two snake species most eagerly sought for pets are the corn snake and the California kingsnake. Both are now available in many mutant colorations and patterns, and most specimens available are the result of captive breedings. Other species of rat, milk, and kingsnakes are also immensely popular with hobbyists. The brown house snake is cyclic in popularity, but is a snake which seems destined for greater hobbyist acceptance. Garter, ribbon, brown, and green snakes are backyard species which are often taken captive when found and are often the first species kept by young enthusiasts. Some garter snakes (including color mutations) are bred in large numbers for pet markets.

Dorsal view of scales on the top of the head.

1. Parietal
2. Postocular
3. Frontal
4. Preocular
5. Loreal
6. Internasal
7. Rostral
8. Temporal
9. Upper labial
10. Supraocular
11. Prefrontal
12. Nasal

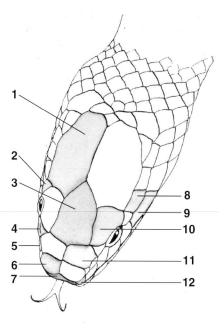

Ventral view of scales on the bottom or chin of a snake.

1. Rostral
2. Anterior chin shield
3. Lower labial
4. Mental
5. Posterior chin shield
6. Ventral

While the head scales of some snakes are fragmented and difficult to identify, the large head scales of most species of harmless snakes are designated in these illustrations.

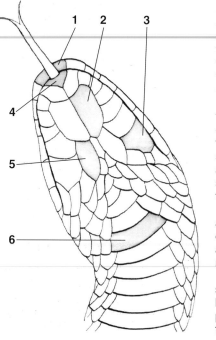

The various colubrines vary from less than 1 foot in length (brown snakes) to more than 8 feet (Neotropical indigos). Most colubrines are somewhere between these lengths. Likewise, most colubrines are very hardy, and some are extremely colorful. Thus they are often thought of as excellent snakes for both beginning and advanced hobbyists.

In addition to those colubrines discussed in this section, there are many others that are readily available to hobbyists. For discussions of some other colubrines, please see the Barron's publications *Corn and Other Rat Snakes* (Bartlett and Bartlett) and *Kingsnakes and Milksnakes* (Markel and Bartlett).

Garter, Ribbon, and Brown Snakes, *Thamnophis* sp.

The garter and ribbon snakes are water-loving, small-bodied natricine snakes of North America. Garter snakes are generally heavier bodied and more terrestrial than the water-loving ribbon snakes. The eastern forms of garter snakes seem to prefer worms, slugs, fish, frogs, and toads, whereas the western forms (and some eastern specimens) add nestling birds, rodents and other snakes and lizards to this diet. Among the favored foods of the ribbon snakes are fish and frogs; some will eat earthworms and slugs. Although most garter snakes are found rather close to water sources, some range rather long distances away from this medium.

Breeding: The American species are ovoviviparous, having large litters of live young. Annual cooling, if not actual extended hibernation, is needed for reproduction.

Comments: Garter and ribbon snakes are active snakes and ready biters. Most are either diurnal or crepuscular, although some aridland forms may be nocturnal. Most thrive (but may not breed successfully) at room temperatures.

On the negative side, if startled, even long-term captive garter snakes will dispel musk from cloacal glands. All have a rather high metabolism and thus require frequent feeding which results, of course, in frequent stooling. This latter translates to frequent cage cleaning. Natricines also enjoy a sizable water dish in which to submerge or fish. While doing the latter, they slide actively through the water, thoroughly dampening their cage. It is important that the cage dry quickly. Use a substrate that dries easily, is easily changed, and discarded.

Common Garter Snake,
Thamnophis sirtalis

The common garter snake is widely distributed across North America. It may be found from the seaside dunes of the Atlantic Ocean to the seaside cliffs of the Pacific. It occurs from coast to coast in southern Canada and from the southernmost tip of the Florida Peninsula to just a few miles north of the United States/Mexico border in California. The common garter snake is, however, absent from the American southwest, northern Montana, southern Saskatchewan, and southern Alberta. Over most of those northern areas it is replaced by the Plains, *T. radix*, and wandering, *T. elegans*, garter snakes.

Certain races (and species) of garter snakes may be incredibly abundant in ideal habitats. The masses of breeding red-sided garter snakes (*T. s. parietalis*) documented by the National Geographic Society (and in other nature films) is one example.

Coloration: The eastern garter snake (*T. s. sirtalis*) is among the most variably colored of all the subspecies of the common garter snake. Typically it is a black(ish) snake boldly patterned with three longitudinal yellow stripes. However, the ground color may vary from olive through gray to tan and the stripes from tan to bluish. In some populations the stripes are lacking (or poorly defined), and a checkerboard pattern is present. Melanistic specimens are commonly found in the Great Lakes region. Albino specimens are fairly common and at least one very brightly colored orange specimen has been found in southeast North Carolina.

The Pacific Coast red-spotted garter snake, *T. s. concinnus*, is one of the most attractive species. It is found in northwest Oregon and extreme southwest Washington. Like many garter snakes it varies in coloration, but may combine ebony, vermilion and lemon in its pattern. The brilliant yellow vertebral stripe is well defined; the lateral stripes are lacking. Some specimens are more subtly colored, lacking much or all of the red and having the lemon replaced by butter yellow.

The **San Francisco garter snake** (*T. s. tetrataenia*) is typified by a solid fire-orange to red-orange dorsolateral

Eastern garter snakes, Thamnophis sirtalis sirtalis, *may have either a striped or checkered pattern. This backyard and old-field snake is the "first snake" for many children.*

The beautiful San Francisco garter snake, Thamnophis sirtalis tetrataenia, *is considered an endangered species that may not be collected or kept captive except by permit.*

central California. This specimen is one of the world's most beautiful snakes; keep in mind, however, that the penalties for harassing or collecting these snakes are harsh.

Checkered Garter Snake, *T. marcianus marcianus*

As might be expected, the checkered garter snake of the southwestern United States and Mexico is named for its checkerboard pattern of black body spots. The neck bears a downward projecting dark blotch on each side. The ground color is olive and if present, the light lateral stripes are pale and wavy.

In nature, the checkered garter snake is most often found along water courses. However, during wet weather, it sometimes wanders far afield. Like other garter snakes, the checkered feeds on amphibians, lizards, minnows, crustaceans, and baby rodents.

Checkered garter snakes thrive in captivity, requiring only a dry cage, a water source, and an ample diet. They have been bred extensively in captivity. Although specimens from the Lower Rio Grande Valley (and other perpetually warm areas) have cycled with only a slight winter cooling and a reduction in the photoperiod, the best success has been achieved by hibernating the snakes.

stripe along each side. It is an endangered subspecies which is now found only in a tiny portion of the remaining marshy habitat on the western San Francisco peninsula of

Ribbon Snakes, *T. proximus* ssp. and *T. sauritus* ssp.

There are only two species of ribbon snakes: the western (*T. proximus*) and the eastern (*T. sauritus*). Each has four subspecies.

Care: Despite their aquatic propensities, ribbon snakes do the best in a primarily dry cage. They do prefer a sizable water container in which they may fish and soak occasionally. They must be able to dry thoroughly between immersings to prevent the

Checkered garter snakes, Thamnophis marcianus, *are now captive bred in both albino, as seen here, and normal color forms.*

onset of skin disorders. Heavy cover in the cage is an *absolute* necessity, due to the nervous nature of these snakes. Security can be provided with live vining plants, plastic foliage, or dried grasses, in combination with horizontal sticks and a small hide box.

Range: The western races are restricted to the central United States, from Wisconsin to New Mexico to Texas to Louisiana, southward to Costa Rica. Collectively, the range of the eastern races embraces all of the eastern one-third of the United States and extreme southern Ontario, Canada.

Appearance: Both species of ribbon snake share a similar appearance. On all ribbon snakes (with the sole possible exception being the Peninsula ribbon snake, *T. s. sackeni*, which may have the vertebral stripe reduced or absent), the stripes are precisely delineated. The eastern species has a dark ventrolateral stripe which involves the outermost tips of the ventral plates. Although present on the western species, the ventrolateral stripe is usually narrower, less well defined, and restricted to the body scales.

It is the western ribbon snake, *T. p. proximus*, that is usually offered for sale. This attractive, graceful snake usually has yellowish side stripes and an orange vertebral stripe. Although it has been known to grow to more than 3 feet in total length, most adults are several inches shorter.

Brown Snakes, *Storeria dekayi* ssp. and Red-Bellied Snakes, *S. occipitmaculata* ssp.

Although secretive, these are two of the most common "fencerow" and vacant lot snakes over much of eastern North America. They may be found and collected from beneath bits of ground debris. Although tiny (8 inches to 1 foot in length), these

Western ribbon snakes, Thamnophis proximus *ssp., are inexpensive and often offered in the pet trade. Unfortunately, nearly all are wild-collected rather than captive bred.*

natricines can show every bit as much spunk as their larger relatives. Their huffs, puffs, and feints are all harmless bluff. They coil, inflate their body with air, flatten their head, and do

Although attractive, the Peninsula ribbon snake, Thamnophis sauritus sackenii, *is not as brightly colored as other races.*

Brown snakes are commonly seen in yards and fields throughout much of their range. They are easily kept worm-eaters. The Florida brown snake, Storeria (dekayi) victa, *seems less frequently encountered than other races.*

their best to look as formidable as is possible for a snake who is less than 1 foot in length. Even a 3-inch neonate will try this type of display.

The beautiful and tiny red-bellied snakes are secretive slug eaters. Pictured is a Florida red-bellied snake, Storeria occipitomaculata obscura.

In captivity, brown snakes will feed on worms; red-bellied snakes will feed on slugs.

Corn and American Rat Snakes

There are six species of New World rat snakes of the genus *Elaphe* and all calm down and eat well in captivity. In this section we will discuss only four—the Baird's rat snake; the corn snake and its western subspecies; the Great Plains rat snake; and the black rat snake and its subspecies. All species may occasionally be found in barns and deserted buildings, roadside dumps, or under other human debris. The eastern species are arboreal and primarily nocturnal.

As their name indicates, these snakes feed primarily on rodents. Their origin, in temperate areas of North America indicates that they won't need a lot of temperature control to do well in captivity. Specimens from colder climes may need hibernation to cycle reproductively, whereas those from the deep south usually require little more than photoperiod manipulation (and even this may not be necessary). Snakes from many generations of captive breeding are easier to breed and cycle than wild-collected specimens.

Baird's Rat Snake, *Elaphe bairdi*

Baird's rat snake is a subtly colored species that is just now gaining in popularity with American hobbyists. Dorsally, adults range from a pearl gray to a dusty orange-brown to a burnt-orange. Adult snakes have four dark to orangish stripes, with the stripes on the back usually being more distinct than those on the sides. The interstitial skin and even the leading edge of each scale may be a bright orange. The venter is usually an unpatterned yellow to orange. The most intensely orange snakes seem to come from the Mexican states of

Nuevo Leon and Tamaulipas, in the southernmost part of the range.

Hatchlings and juveniles are grayish with a busy pattern of many thin dorsal saddles. There are numerous, well-defined lateral blotches. A curved dark bar crosses the snout immediately anterior to the eyes, and a dark diagonal postocular stripe runs from eye to mouth. With maturity, both markings pale, and eventually disappear completely. The head of an adult Baird's rat snake does not have any markings.

Size: This is a moderately heavily-bodied snake with a maximum size of just over 5 feet; females are generally longer than the males.

Range: Baird's rat snake is found southward from central Texas, in disjunct areas, to northeastern Mexico.

Reproduction: Although these snakes seem to reproduce best if hibernated, our pairs produced viable eggs with little more than a slight winter cooling and a reduction of photoperiod. Hatchlings are about 1 foot in length. Clutches number from 4–10 eggs. Hatching occurs after about 2½ months at an incubation temperature of 82–86°F (28–29°C). The hatchlings almost always feed readily on newly born mice. Large, healthy females can produce two clutches annually.

Comments: Both the Mexican and Texas color morphs are now being bred by hobbyists. The Mexican differs from the Texas specimens by a gray head and a ground color suffused with orange. With captive breeding, these once rather expensive snakes are now being seen with increasing frequency—and at decreasing prices.

Baird's rat snake (named after Spencer Fullerton Baird, a 19th-century vertebrate zoologist) was originally considered a subspecies of the very wide-ranging *E. obsoleta.* Baird's is an attractive, easily handled, very hardy rat snake.

Baird's rat snake, Elaphe bairdi, *is subtly but attractively colored.*

Corn Snake, *E. gutatta gutatta*

Few snake hobbyists need any introduction to the corn snake. This medium-sized (6 feet for a very large specimen), red-on-gray or red-on-orange blotched snake of the southeastern United States is probably the most popular snake in captivity and has been bred in captivity for more than 40 years.

Extensive corn snake breeding programs have added more than 20 colors and patterns to the normal blotched phase. However, many hobbyists have commented to us that they think nothing is more attractive than the common, normal, corn snake.

But there's still a lot of color variety in the term "normal." We consider "normal" to be any color phase occurring in the wild in sufficient numbers as to form a viable, sustainable population. The Okeetee, Miami, and Hastings phase corn snakes are "normals," as are the dark anerythristic corn snakes from southwest Florida and the rosy rat snakes from the Florida Keys. Although two other

This specimen of the corn snake, Elaphe guttata guttata, *a species variable even in nature, was found in northeastern Florida. Hobbyists call this the "Hastings phase."*

phases, the blood red and albino corn, have been found in the wild, neither seems to be found in sufficient numbers to constitute a population.

In the authors' opinion, the Okeetee phase corn snake outshines all others in brilliance.

Okeetee phase corn snakes are noted for their brilliance. Bright scarlet saddles, broadly edged with jet black, are set against a vibrant red-orange ground color. This is the naturally occurring color phase found in eastern Georgia, South Carolina, and North Carolina. Beyond (and even within) this geographic region, colors may vary and be less intense.

Anerythristic: Despite rampant and habitat modifying development, southwest Florida remains a popular location for anerythristic corn snakes (corn snakes that lack the red pigment). This color phase, also called "black albino" and "melanistic" by hobbyists, has black or deep brown saddles on a gray background and often has a yellow or peach wash on the sides of the neck. However, except for the black "corn snake spearpoint" on the head, the snake is more reminiscent of a black rat snake than a corn snake.

Blood red: These morphs were originally found among normally colored individuals in northeastern Florida. The name refers to the snake's deep red coloration. Sadly, the hatchlings of the blood red corn snakes are among the most difficult to induce to feed, and even once started, not all thrive. Problems have continued, even with outbreeding followed by a subsequent redevelopment of the red strain. If you are considering buying this morph, watch the snake feed before you buy it.

Miami phase: Although the Miami phase corn snake is a very different, less lauded creature than the coveted Okeetee phase, it too, is beautiful and hardy. Its "maroon on pearl-gray or silver" coloration is a familiar sight over much of the southern third of the Florida peninsula. This amazingly resilient snake persists even amidst the rubble-surrounded warehouse complexes of downtown Miami.

In some areas of Florida, rather extensive populations of anerythristic (lacking red) corn snakes exist.

Several color variants of the corn snake occur in the Florida Keys. These were once called rosy rat snakes.

Rosy rat snake: The term "rosy rat snake" is a hobbyist's designation for the small, faded corn snakes of the Florida Keys. Once thought to be a rather standardized pale rose on rose color with a little black in the patterning, we now realize that these are actually very color varied snakes. Other phases include the orange (rosy ground color with orange blotches), the olive (olive-drab ground with an army blanket green wash on the head and orange blotches), the silver (gray to gun-metal blue ground with red-orange blotches), and the chocolate (brownish ground with orange blotches). Many of these phases have been refined and per-petuated by John Decker, a rosy rat snake specialist breeder in Hollywood, Florida. (For those who might wish to collect their own specimens, be aware that the corn snakes of the lower Florida Keys are now protected by Florida law.)

Designer Corn Snakes: The follow-ing names all refer to herpetoculturally derived color phases of the corn snake: Sunglow, amelansitic Okeetee, candy-

cane, snow, ghost, blizzard, Christmas, caramel, mocha, and butter.

Other names, such as zigzag or zipper, motley or mottled, and striped, refer to pattern anomalies.

The name "creamsicle" has been coined for the beautiful amelanistic cross between the corn and the Great

Creamsicle corn snakes were produced by intergrading a corn snake, E. g. guttata, with a Great Plains rat snake, E. guttata emoryi.

Plains rat snake. This is a beautiful yellow-white snake with peach to pale-orange blotches. The color usually intensifies with advancing age.

Great Plains Rat Snake, *E. guttata emoryi*

The Great Plains rat snake is currently the only valid subspecies of the corn snake. It looks much like a corn snake but with dark gray saddles on a gray-to-olive-gray background.

Size: The Great Plains rat snake seldom exceeds 4.5 feet in length, and the record length is only 5¼ inches.

Range: It is common in our central states and in northeastern Mexico.

Reproduction: Because most Great Plains rat snakes originate from cooler areas than corn snakes, a period of actual hibernation may be required to cycle them for breeding. A reduction in winter temperature (to 45–52°F) and photoperiod for 70 to 90 days is recommended. (See pages 26–27 for more details on hibernation techniques.)

Because they are so outshone by the red colors of the more easterly corn snake, not many hobbyists seek out the Great Plains rat snake. It certainly is less popular in captive-breeding programs than its eastern cousin. However, it was through the intergrading of the Great Plains rat snake and the corn snake that the spectacular "creamsicle corn" was developed. Although wild albino Great Plains rat snakes have been found, most of those now seen in captivity have albino corn snake genes somewhere in their background.

Food: The adult corn snake and the Great Plains rat snake feed primarily on rodents, but the diet in the wild (especially for the younger snakes) includes bats, birds, lizards, and frogs. The prey is killed by constriction.

Black Rat Snake, *E. o. obsoleta*

Even though of a dark color and hence less visually appealing than some of its other subspecies, the black rat snake is a favorite of many beginning reptile enthusiasts.

Coloration: The normal coloration of the black rat snake varies considerably over its wide range. The darkest (blackest) individuals seem to come from the northeast and the mountains of the southeast. Specimens that we have found in the southern Blue Ridge Mountains have been as dark as specimens we have found in the Berkshires of Massachusetts. On the other hand, black rat snakes from the western part of the range are often more brown than black. The largest individuals tend to be the darkest. Under bright lighting, the dark blotches of babyhood are still usually seen. It is the light ground color that becomes suffused with melanin, finally obscuring the dorsal blotching. The interstitial skin may be lighter, being white or reddish, and the throat is light (often white). The chin coloration may extend for a variable distance onto the venter.

Variants: At least two genetically distinct albino forms of the black rat

Despite a lack of bright colors, the black rat snake, Elaphe obsoleta obsoleta, *is an interesting, large constrictor that is now captive bred in both normal and albino morphs.*

snake are now available. To add additional variety, albino intergrades between black rat snakes and other races have been developed. These are now available to hobbyists under names which may—or may not—reflect their lineage.

A brindle black rat snake has been developed and a "bubblegum" variant, an albino hybrid between Everglades, yellow, and black rat snakes, is readily available. Ads for these latter claim that "no two are identical," and the ads may be right!

Size: The black rat snake is the largest of the several subspecies and with a record size of 101 inches it is one of the largest snakes in the United States.

Range: The black rat snake is the northeasternmost member of the group. It ranges from the southern tip of Ontario, southern Massachusetts, and southeastern Minnesota, southward to northern Louisiana and central Georgia. It is not usually found in the coastal plain of the Carolinas where it is replaced by the smaller but the more brightly colored yellow rat snake.

Breeding: These snakes do well either with or without a period of winter dormancy; although those from northern areas seem to need winter dormancy for reproduction. Most feed readily year-round if kept warm. Captive-breeding supplies most of the specimens available in the pet market, thus lessening the number of specimens taken from the wild. All the obsoleta are oviparous, and most can attain sexual maturity in their second summer. Small and young specimens have fewer and smaller eggs than older, larger adults. The clutch of an old, healthy female (anywhere from 3 years of age and up) often contains 25 or more eggs. The eggs are easily incubated and hatched, and the hatchling snakes are robust and easily reared. The hatchlings of the black rat snake have dark saddles on a deep-gray (gray rat snake) to pinkish (Everglades rat snake) ground color. Hatchlings can exceed 1 foot in length and some of 16 inches in length have been reported.

Subspecies: The black rat snake has some very well-known subspecies. Perhaps the best known is the yellow rat snake (*E. o. quadrivittata*).

Yellow Rat Snake, *E. o. quadrivittata*

The adult yellow rat snake has a variably yellow or yellow-green ground color. Most have four prominent dark lines. This subspecies ranges southward along the coastal plain from just south of North Carolina's Albemarle Peninsula to the central Florida Keys.

The most intensely colored specimens occur on the extreme south of peninsula Florida to the region of Big Pine Key. These were once referred to as **Deckert's** or **Keys rat snakes.** This variant retains the juvenile saddles throughout its life, but, also develops stripes with age. The ground color may be yellow-orange, deep orange, or brownish-orange, and the tongue is black. The saddles can be prominent

Yellow rat snakes, Elaphe obsoleta quadrivittata, *are large, hardy, and powerful constrictors that are commonly seen in the southeastern United States and breed readily in captivity.*

or vague and of a brownish to maroon color. The most attractive animals are those with the deep orange ground color and maroon saddles. Apparently this snake has never been common. Today, a Keys variant yellow rat snake is considered much harder to find than the "rosy rat" corn snake.

Albino yellow rat snakes have been collected and are being bred. Albino specimens retain the saddles; the stripes are poorly defined.

Intergrades: The "**greenish rat snake**" is a naturally occurring intergrade between the yellow and the black rat snakes. It is common where the ranges of the two subspecies abut in areas of Georgia, extreme southern South Carolina, and on northward to southeastern Tennessee. Often of a dingy olive color when adult, the four stripes are usually prominent.

The **Gulf Hammock** rat snake of northwestern peninsular Florida is also a naturally occurring intergrade between the gray rat and the yellow rat snakes. Of grayish ground color, this snake retains the juvenile saddles and develops the usual yellow rat four stripes.

Everglades Rat Snake, *E. o. rossalleni*

The **Everglades rat snake** is the most colorful subspecies. These are big orange snakes with obscure striping. When the Everglades really was the Everglades, rather than limitless expanses of sod and sugarcane farms, Everglades rat snakes were common in inland Florida from south of Lake Okeechobee to Monroe County. Because of intergradation with the yellow rat snake which followed the draining of the Everglades inland and southward, true Everglades rat snakes are now nearly impossible to find. The body, head, chin, and eyes are an (often rich) orange. The tongue is entirely red. (Black tongue pigment would indicate a "visiting" yellow rat snake in the fairly recent lineage.) Everglades rat snakes can exceed 6 feet in total length.

Captive breeding successes: Does this mean that Everglades rat snakes are gone entirely? Fortunately, no. Through selective breeding, herpetoculturists have kept this race alive and well—perhaps even enhanced. Not only are Everglades rat snakes produced each year, but a **hypomelanistic** phase has been developed. With the reduction of the melanin, the body color of these adults is a resplendent red-orange. This snake looks more like what we think an albino ought to look like than the albinos themselves do.

Other morphs: Another project involving Everglades snakes has produced a recessive blotchless phase. Not even the hatchlings have the normal dorsal blotches. Other striped subspecies have been worked in here, and the phase is now available in normally pigmented and amelanistic morphs.

The Everglades rat snake, Elaphe obsoleta rossalleni, *is now difficult to find in the wild. However, they are captive bred in large numbers.*

Gray Rat Snake, *E. o. spiloides*

The **gray rat snake** is the deep south's lighter colored version of the north's black rat snake. Actually, there are two color phases of the gray rat snake—the rather dark, gray-on-gray **"normal phase"** and the lighter, more attractive gray on grayish-white **"white-oak phase."** The dark dorsal saddles (which this subspecies retains throughout its life) are often bordered with an even darker, narrow edging; those of the white oak phase are often narrowly edged with a very light gray. The saddles may be completely dark or light centered. The biggest recorded gray rat was 84.25 inches. Gray rat snakes may be encountered from coastal panhandle Florida to western Missouri. From there they range northward to northern Alabama and in the somewhat warmer Mississippi River valley to extreme western Kentucky, southeastern Illinois, and immediately adjacent Indiana.

Texas Rat Snake, *E. o. lindhiemerii*

The **Texas rat snake** was named for herpetologist Fred Lindheimer. Its distinguishing characteristic is its belligerence. We don't know of another nonvenomous snake in the United States that so readily bites, or none which strikes so many times in rapid succession. To add insult to injury, this is not an attractive snake. It retains its blotches throughout its life, and it's lighter than a black rat and darker than a gray rat. The ground color can vary from straw-yellow to orange, but usually is tan or light brown. The dorsal blotches are rather elongate, fairly narrow and medium to deep brown, either with or without light centers. The contrast between the dark dorsal blotches and the lighter ground color is not very great. The lateral interstitial skin can vary from yellow to orange. The interstitial color may spill over onto the lead-

Not all Texas rat snakes, Elaphe obsoleta lindheimerii, *are as prettily colored as this specimen.*

ing edges of some lateral scales, but since the trailing edge of the preceding scales overlaps, the little brilliance may not be seen unless the snake is distended with food or tightly coiled.

Other morphs: Actually, few hobbyists work with normal, wild-caught Texas rat snakes. However, many do keep and breed two of the most common mutants—an albino (actually amelanistic rather than a true albino) and a leucistic. Of the two, the albino is the less attractive, being white (almost translucent when hatched) with pink saddles. The colors intensify somewhat with increasing age. The dorsal saddles of older adults are usually pale strawberry. The eyes of the amelanistic are pink.

The leucistic morph is a beautiful creature. It is a solid, unpatterned white and has gray-blue eyes.

A Few Old World Rat Snakes

Despite being thought to be more delicate and thus more "difficult" than their U.S. relatives, a few Old World rat snakes are now becoming popular in the U.S. pet trade.

The Asiatic radiated rat snake, Elaphe radiata, *is a pretty species that is typically endowed with a rather bad disposition.*

Certainly, wild-collected Old World rat snakes **can** be more nervous and harder to handle than captive-bred specimens. As a precaution, wild-caught specimens should be examined for endoparasites as soon as possible; parasitic infections that were once considered life threatening to the snakes are now easily treated. Most Old World rat snakes are also relatively slow to attain maturity. From hatchling size, it may take 3 years for many to reach sexual maturity.

Although the Old World rat snakes are as effective constrictors as their U.S. counterparts, many immobilize a prey item by grasping it in their mouth and then throwing a single loop of their body over it.

Radiated (or Copperhead) Rat Snake, *E. radiata*

Coloration: Unlike many of its Asian congenerics, the radiated rat snake is striped *anteriorly*, rather than posteriorly. The four stripes—two heavy dorsolateral stripes and two much thinner lateral stripes—are best defined on the anterior trunk. The ground color of *E. radiata* may vary from buff, tan, light brown or coppery-russet, to yellowish or greenish. The three dark stripes radiating from the eye and the dark collar (with which the uppermost of the orbital stripes connects) are representative of the species.

Hypomelanistic (lacking much melanin), anerythristic (lacking all red pigment), and albino specimens are also available.

Behavior: Wild-caught adults of this Asian rat snake are very defensive. Even when vaguely threatened, the radiated esses its neck, inflates its throat, and vigorously strikes to defend itself. Because adults can grow to more than 6 feet in length, the striking range is fairly extensive. However, this snake, which acts quite racer-like, would rather flee than fight. If neither fleeing nor aggressive behavior work, a frightened radiated rat snake may then play dead, writhing, rolling over, and partially opening the mouth and extending the tongue. It may then remain immobile for several minutes. They will tame down with handling.

Range: The radiated rat snake is found over a vast section of southeast Asia.

Breeding: It is only recently that these nervous rat snakes have been captive bred in the United States. Until then, *all* available specimens were wild-collected imports. They do not seem to require even a period of cooling to cycle reproductively. However, a natural photoperiod does seem to help. Egg clutches of *E. radiata* consist usually of three to nine eggs, but sometimes more than 20 are laid by large, healthy females. Females are known to have several clutches during a single season. The hatchlings are usually 10 inches in total length.

Diet: Some wild-collected *E. radiata* can be problematic feeders. Housing them in sizable, quiet terraria with ample hiding areas may help. Offer reluctant feeders a variety of prey items, including a small rat, a large mouse, a small hamster or gerbil, or a baby chick or quail. Captive-bred radiated rat snakes and even wild-collected babies will usually readily accept mice.

Amur (Russian) Rat Snake, E. schrencki schrencki

Coloration: In coloration, adult Amur rat snakes are much like the more familiar eastern kingsnake. Both appear as black snakes patterned with numerous pale crossbands (in reality, it is the light pigment which is the ground color). The labials (lip scales) and chin are light, often a rather bright yellow with black scale-seams. The yellowish color may also appear beneath the tail. The belly may be either heavily patterned or unpatterned. Young Amur rat snakes are prominently marked with dark-edged brown dorsal saddles and tan to gray crossbars. A dark bar begins just posterior to the nostril, extends through the eye and angles downward to the angle of the jaw.

Captive care: Amur rat snakes are one of the calmest and easiest of the Old World rat snakes to keep. They readily feed on rodents. Most adults feed on prey up to the size of medium rats. Amur rat snakes are large (often to 5 feet, rarely to 6 feet) and are fairly heavily bodied.

Because of their northerly range, captive Amur rat snakes do not require a lot of auxiliary heat. A cage temperature of 72–76°F with an illuminated basking spot of 82–85°F is satisfactory.

Breeding: Hibernation is a necessary part of reproductive cycling. Although a hibernation of up to 5 months has been suggested for Amur rat snakes, our snakes bred well (and regularly) with a standardized 90-day hibernation period. Hibernating snakes were cooled to between 47 and 52°F. They were awakened for a drink at 2–3 week intervals. Clutches had from 7–16 eggs. The foot-long babies would hatch after close to 60 days of incubation at 77–82°F. Following (sometimes even before) their postnatal shed, hatchlings are usually voracious feeders on small mice.

Both subspecies of the Asiatic Elaphe schrencki *are now available in herpetoculture. The Korean rat snake,* E. s. anomala, *top, retains the juvenile pattern while the Amur rat snake,* E. s. schrencki, *bottom, darkens noticeably with age.*

73

Range: *E. s. schrencki* is found in Siberia, Manchuria, and northeastern Korea.

Subspecies: *E. s. anomala* is a lighter colored, usually more nervous, more southerly subspecies. It occurs from western Korea to northeastern China. Although it is less frequently seen in the U.S. pet trade, when available it is often referred to as the Korean rat snake. It has a ground color of tan, olive-tan, or olive-gray, which is brightest posteriorly. The blotches are only vaguely darker and may be represented by only their outlines of buff. The blotches, when present, are usually better defined (and darker) toward the tailtip.

Leopard Snake, *E. situla*

Coloration: The leopard snake is one of the most beautiful members of the entire genus. It vaguely resembles the corn snake. However, the two are actually *very* different. The "saddles" of the leopard rat snake are actually two rows of dark-edged strawberry, dorsolateral spots, some of which may, or may not, be connected vertebrally by dorsal extensions. The ground color of the leopard rat snake may be gray, olive-gray, tan, or pale olive-green. The head pattern is rather complex. A dark bar extends across the top of the head immediately anterior to the eyes. The top of the head is patterned with a black-outlined red blotch extending anteriorly from the forked neck blotch to a point just posterior to the eyes. A diagonal black temporal stripe is present on both sides.

Size: The leopard rat snake is the smallest of the European rat snakes. An average size for adults is between 26 and 30 inches.

Range and habitat: This species ranges from eastern Turkey westward to Yugoslavia, and to eastern and southern Italy and Sicily. A disjunct population occurs in Ukraine, on the Crimean Peninsula. *E. situla* is associated with hot, dry, often sandy, rocky, or sparsely wooded habitats. Like its European congeners, the leopard rat snake prefers fencerows, ruins, and old stone walls.

Diet: Like many of the small and slender rat snakes of the world, *E. situla* prefers small meals of nestling rodents and ground dwelling birds. Hatchlings and juveniles may feed on lizards and tree frogs. Our specimens have had heavy amounts of endoparasites and were initially reluctant to feed on anything but wild mice (*Peromyscus*).

Caging: Our leopard rat snakes are now housed in pairs or trios in a 20-gallon terraria that has a substrate of fallen leaves atop 1–2 inches of sandy soil. Several secure hiding places are in each cage. Leopard rat snakes are calm snakes and do not often bite. The temperature varies, but during the summer is usually between 82 and 88°F by day on the illuminated end

The prettiest of the European rat snakes, is Elaphe situla, *the leopard rat snake. Often referred to as a corn snake lookalike, the leopard rat snake is uncommon in American herpetoculture.*

and several degrees cooler on the dark end. Night temperatures are allowed to decrease by several degrees. Winter temperatures on the cool end of the terrarium by day are in the mid-60s to very low seventies. After the basking light is turned off in the late afternoon, the entire tank cools.

We had been cautioned that preparing a suitable hibernaculum for these snakes would be difficult. This did not prove true. They survived the winter well under standard conditions. The snakes were roused at 2-week intervals for a lengthy drink.

Breeding: We have had several pairs of second-generation captive-bred leopard rat snakes breed successfully without having undergone hibernation. These individuals have experienced winter cooling as well as a natural photoperiod throughout the year.

The clutches produced by this species are small—each clutch consisting of only two to eight eggs. Incubation takes about 60 days at 77–82°F. Hatchlings measure close to 1 foot in length and will generally begin feeding on mice soon after the postnatal shed.

Comments: Because of their great beauty and comparative rarity, leopard rat snakes are coveted by collectors. Expensive even in Europe, the few that are sold in the United States may be very expensive. Yet, they are of immense interest and well worth the somewhat specialized care that they require to thrive.

Subspecies: No subspecies are currently recognized.

Striped-Tailed Rat Snakes, E. taeniura

Coloration: The several poorly differentiated blotched races of this attractive species are often referred to as beauty snakes. This is often prefixed with an origin such as "Taiwan," "Chinese," or "Yunnan." The more rarely seen striped subspecies are often called cave rat snakes. Subspecies can be difficult to identify positively.

It is only three of the blotched races that are currently seen with any regularity in the U.S. pet trade. Both color and pattern vary on all. These are the:

Although wild-collected specimens can be delicate and bad-tempered, captive-hatched and raised striped-tailed rat snakes, Elaphe taeniura, are hardy and easily handled. Pictured are an intergrade Yunnan x Taiwan striped-tailed rat snake, E. t. yunnanensis x E. t. friesi, top, and an unidentified form, bottom, now being shipped from Vietnam.

1. Taiwan striped-tailed rat snake (*E. t. friesei*). This race seems to differ only in the *average* number of ventral scales (243–262) from the nominate form.

2. Chinese striped-tailed rat snake (*E. t. taeniura*) occurs on the Chinese mainland, Burma, and Thailand. The number of ventral scales on this race varies from 225–255.

3. Yunnan striped-tailed rat snake (*E. t. yunnanensis*) (=*vaillanti*) is a (usually) more pallid and poorly patterned subspecies. It occurs in Yunnan Province, China.

The many races of *E. taeniura* vary tremendously in appearance. Some (*taeniura* and *friesei*) are proportionately heavy bodied, strongly blotched anteriorly, striped posteriorly, and have a ground color of olive-buff to olive-yellow-green. *E. t. yunnanensis* (=*vaillanti*) is intermediate in appearance between the heavy, blotched forms and the attenuate racer-like subspecies. *E. t. vaillanti* tends to have less well-defined, double anterior body blotches or, if single, the blotches are usually narrow vertebrally.

Range: The three subspecies described above are only found in China. Other subspecies range southward from northern China throughout most of southeast Asia to Sumatra. They may be found from sea level to near 11,000 feet.

Breeding: All three of the above subspecies are now being bred in U.S. herpetoculture. Some breeders use 90 days of actual hibernation, whereas others use just a cooling period.

Females lay up to 14 (usually 6–10) eggs per clutch. At 80°F, incubation lasts for about 60 days. Hatchlings are very large, often being more than 16 inches in total length. They feed on furred baby mice.

Size: All races of this snake commonly attain a length of more than 6 feet. The published record size for *E.*

t. friesei is 7 feet 9 inches but specimens of more than 5.5 feet are fairly uncommon.

Captive care: Our *E. taeniura* specimens have seemed most content when kept cool. Terrarium temperature is usually 70–76°F (21–24°C). An illuminated basking area set at about 86°F (29°C) is provided. When keeping and breeding the various races of this snake, err toward coolness rather than heat. The snakes only sometimes avail themselves of the warmth, especially if "traffic" is heavy near their cage.

We consider all of the various subspecies rather nervous but easily kept. They are moderately difficult to breed.

Kingsnakes and Milksnakes

Although they are quite closely allied to the rat and the gopher snakes, milksnakes and the kingsnakes are very different in appearance and actions. Milksnakes and kingsnakes are more secretive, usually have heads only slightly larger than their neck, are quite cannibalistic, and many are resistant to the venoms of pit vipers.

Baby milksnakes and kingsnakes are more prone to cannibalism than the adults, but it is best to house both milksnakes and kingsnakes of all sizes separately. It is especially important to feed these snakes separately.

Besides other snakes, in the wild, milksnakes and kingsnakes eat amphibians, lizards and their eggs, hatchling turtles and turtle eggs, and suitably sized rodents. Most captives will adapt well to a diet exclusively of lab rodents.

Milksnakes are one of the most brightly colored snakes. Most are clad in rings of red, black, and yellow (or white). Gaudy when seen in a cage, when in the wild and moving, these snakes blend surprisingly well with their backgrounds.

When encountered in the wild, milk-snakes and kingsnakes may draw their necks into an "S" and strike animatedly. Despite this initial show of bravado, kingsnakes usually quiet down and become less belligerent after only a few handlings. On the other hand, most milksnakes remain nervous and may resent handling throughout their lives. Despite this, their beauty endears them to many hobbyists, and they are among the most eagerly sought snakes.

Although we don't consider these snakes as satisfying captives as rat and gopher snakes, brisk sales at reptile shows and pet shops show that many hobbyists think otherwise.

The eastern kingsnake, Lampropeltis getula getula, *is one of the larger and more attractively marked of its group.*

Common King Snake, *Lampropeltis getula* ssp.

Eastern Kingsnake *Lampropeltis g. getola*: Because of the chain-like pattern of white or cream markings against the shiny black or deep brown ground color, the large (to 82 inches), robust, nominate form is often referred to as the "chain king."

Hatchlings may have a considerable amount of strawberry red or russet along their flanks. There are albino forms.

The eastern kingsnake is found in suitable habitats from central New Jersey southward to northern Florida and westward to the Appalachians and southeastern Alabama. It tames readily in captivity and feeds well on rodents.

Adult females lay from 6–12 eggs. Except for the red on their flanks, hatchlings are diminutive replicas of the adults. They are hardy, feeding easily and growing rapidly.

California Kingsnake, *L. g. californiae*

This moderately sized (3.5–4.25 feet) snake is, to the kingsnake breeders, what the corn snake is to rat

snake breeders. They make good pets once they adjust to captivity. Although naturally somewhat variable, "Cal kings," as they are called by hobbyists, are now available to collectors in many hues and patterns that Mother Nature never imagined. Albinos may be more commonly seen than "normally" colored specimens.

Albino California kingsnakes are now mass-produced in captive breeding facilities. This is a striped phase albino.

In the wild, it is the banded phase of the California kingsnake, Lampropeltis getula californiae, *that is most often seen. The ground color varies from brown to black and the bands from narrow to wide.*

"Normal" California kingsnakes are banded in white or cream against a black or deep-brown ground. The bands may continue around the belly, or the belly may be primarily dark or light. The stark black and white specimens are often referred to as the "desert phase" and were once thought to represent a separate, now unrecognized, subspecies—*yumensis.*

In this captive produced phase of the California kingsnake, the white dominates the black.

Like all kingsnakes, the Cal king is a powerful constrictor and an opportunistic feeder. It will eat amphibians, reptiles (including baby turtles and snakes), small ground-nesting birds, and small mammals. Captives feed on lab mice.

Breeding: Well-fed Cal kings grow rapidly and may be large and old enough to breed in their second year of life. Most will definitely breed in their third year. Males, which grow more slowly than the females, can breed successfully at a younger age than the females.

After having been captive bred for several generations, the "domestic" offspring are easier to cycle reproductively than wild-collected specimens. After having reached sexual maturity, our captive-produced Cal kings have cycled and produced large clutches of viable eggs with no more preparation than a natural photoperiod and a good body weight. Large, healthy females may produce a second clutch of eggs. On the other hand, we have not successfully bred wild-collected specimens without hibernating them.

Variants: We mentioned earlier the desert phase and the normal colored and patterned California kingsnakes. A few other herpetocultural variants include:

1. 50/50: Dark and light colorations are of nearly equal extent with a variable pattern that usually combines partial striping with banding. A banana (or high yellow) of enhanced brilliance has also been developed.

2. The striped pattern, rather uncommon in nature, has been perpetuated by captive-breeding programs.

3. The southern Baja Peninsula is home to a California kingsnake with a poorly defined, *very* narrow, often cinnamon vertebral stripe. This was once known as *L. g. nitida* and is still referred to as the South Baja *"nitida"* phase by hobbyists. Further north on the peninsula we encounter the mid-Baja "conjuncta" phase. This phase has very narrow, poorly defined light banding. On some dark specimens, in subdued lighting, the banding may be barely discernible. A rather similar appearing animal, usually called "melanistic" by hobbyists is found in mid-California.

Some Natural Florida Intergrade Kingsnakes

Because taxonomists and hobbyists interpret the concept of "species" and "subspecies" differently, the views of the two often differ sharply. This is the case when the **"Apalachicola Lowland"** (=**Blotched**) Kingsnake (*L. g. getula* x *L.g. floridana*) is being discussed. To hobbyists, this tremendously variable form will always be the "blotched" kingsnake to which the scientific name of "*L. g. goini*" is attached. As currently understood by biologists, the species is merely variable intergrade between the Florida and the eastern kingsnakes. The exact genetics of this attractive and variable kingsnake remains conjectural and will stay so until studies, currently underway, are completed. Found in Gulf and Calhoun Counties, Florida, the blotched form is only one color and pattern extreme of a very variable kingsnake. In fact, this coveted snake of the northern Florida hinterlands displays nearly as much variation as the better known California kingsnake. However, when a vertebral stripe is present, it is dark rather than light.

The Apalachicola Lowland kingsnake is large and robust. Captives have grown to 6 feet in length, exceeding the longest recorded wild specimen by more than 4 inches.

The hatchlings of the Apalachicola Lowland kingsnake are usually darker or redder than the adults. They feed

The lineage of the very variable Apalachicola Lowland kingsnake, Lampropeltis getula ssp., remains muddled. At the moment it is considered a naturally occurring intergrade of the eastern and the Florida kingsnakes.

readily and grow rapidly. Normal clutch size is from 6–12 eggs.

The **Peninsula Intergrade Kingsnake,** another intergradation between *L. g. floridana* and *L. g. getula*, was once known as the Florida kingsnake and is still called this by most breeders and pet trade

Hatchlings of the Apalachicola Lowland kingsnake are often strongly suffused with orange. Normally this fades with growth. However, a line of these snakes has now been developed which retains the orange throughout their lives.

Most of the kingsnakes of peninsular Florida are now considered naturally occurring intergrades of the eastern x the Florida kingsnakes.

operators. This snake is a hardy and prolific captive, feeding well, growing rapidly, quieting quickly, and breeding readily. These interesting snakes have a light to dark brown ground coloration with numerous (22–66) cream to yellow crossbands. Light spots on the dark body scales can impart a vaguely speckled appearance. Hatchlings may

The snake now recognized as the Florida kingsnake, Lampropeltis getula floridana, *was long referred to as the South Florida or Brook's king. It is typified by a busy but faded pattern and a yellowish coloration.*

have considerable red on the flanks but are otherwise similar to the adults.

This is one of the few kingsnakes in which the wild-collected specimens still seem to outnumber the captive bred and born hatchlings in the pet trade.

Intergrade kingsnakes may occasionally exceed 5 feet in length.

Florida Kingsnake, *L. g. floridana*

This race of the common kingsnake is confusing to many hobbyists. These snakes are the variably colored, but often quite yellow, kingsnakes that were once called *L. g. brooksi.* Dealers and hobbyists are still quite likely to call them "Brook's kingsnakes."

These pale-colored snakes of the oolitic limestone prairies of extreme south Florida are coveted by hobbyists. These snakes are avidly sought by herpetoculturists and bring the highest prices to their breeders. All color phases make good pets.

Is the Florida kingsnake rare in the wild? Not really. What is rare, however, are the very palest morphs that are so eagerly sought by hobbyists. These palest specimens are usually found ONLY on the high and dry, exposed, pock-marked, white oolitic limestone excrescences. Specimens found virtually next to them in the mucklands of the southern Everglades are considerably darker. Even in the choicest habitat, color variation is apparent.

The Florida kingsnake, as now understood, is somewhat smaller than its conspecifics from further north. A length of 4 feet is commonly attained and Conant/Collins report a 69.5 foot record size. Males seem to be larger and of lighter color.

Clutch size ranges from 4–12, and the robust hatchlings are much darker than the adults. Like many of the eastern kingsnakes, hatchlings may have considerable red on the sides. This fades to the adult coloration after a few sheds.

Although several other subspecies of the eastern kingsnake are available in the pet trade, they are not as popular. The black king, *L. g. nigra*, of the highlands of southeastern United States is perhaps the least popular of the remaining forms. It is very similar to, but darker than, the speckled kingsnake, *L. g. holbrooki* of the Mississippi Valley and associated drainages. Both of these are prone to unpleasant dispositions and are more predisposed than other races to cannibalism. The desert king, *L. g. splendida*, is the most attractive of these several forms. It is a species of the Chihuahuan desert of the United States and northern Mexico. The Mexican black king, *L. g. nigritus*, may be vaguely patterned or jet black. It is of fairly placid disposition and, because of the many similarities between it and the California kingsnake, a fair amount of interest is shown by hobbyists.

Comments: Although in the east and in other normally moist regions kingsnakes may be encountered some distance from water, in more arid areas they are associated with swamp, marsh, or riveredge habitats. In addition to the foods mentioned here, these powerful constrictors will overpower and consume native venomous snake species. Despite this, kingsnakes are not the dedicated enemies of venomous snakes as many people think.

Milk and Scarlet Kingsnakes, *L. triangulum* ssp.

No snake book would be complete without mention of these remarkably beautiful, hardy, and popular snakes. This section will give you only an idea of the variety in this group. (For more information see *Kingsnakes and Milksnakes: A Complete Pet Care Manual* by Markel and Bartlett.) The

The Andean milksnake, Lampropeltis triangulum andesiana, *is a very large subspecies that is brilliant as a hatchling, but often darkens with advancing age.*

only disadvantage of having these snakes is their slight nervousness and their need to privacy and seclusion.

The very variable **Honduran milksnake,** *L. t. hondurensis*, is one of the most popular of the tropical American forms. It occurs in a typical black, yellow, and red-ringed milk snake form as well as a startling red-orange, black and orange-banded "tangerine"

The Sinaloan milksnake, Lampropeltis triangulum sinaloae, *is one of the most beautiful and precisely marked of the many subspecies.*

The tangerine, top, and the milksnake, bottom, phases of the Honduran milksnake, Lampropeltis triangulum hondurensis, *are naturally occurring color variants.*

Herpetoculturists are striving to develop pattern, top, and color, albino specimen, bottom, aberrancies of the Honduran milksnake.

form. Albinos are now available to hobbyists but at expensive prices.

Adult *hondurensis* generally exceed a fairly heavy 3.5 feet in total length; a very few may grow to five feet. Healthy hatchlings can exceed 15 feet in length, and usually feed readily on pinky mice.

Caging: Like all milksnakes (all members of the genus, in fact) Honduran milks are secretive snakes.

They ably find their way beneath surface debris, both of natural and man-made origin, and are fully capable of making their own tunnels in loose soils. They are very good escape artists, and their constant nudging habits enable them to find the weakest point of caging. Cage them *securely!*

A thick substrate of cypress mulch, aspen shavings, or fallen leaves, ensures that the snakes will feel secure, but negates easy viewing of the snakes. Because of this, milksnakes of all kinds are less satisfactory pet snakes than many snakes of other genera. However, if you can enjoy them under conditions when they feel secure, they make very suitable pets.

Hiding boxes and furniture of fallen limbs or secured rocks will also be appreciated by the snakes. By keeping the snakes on a substrate of newspaper with a hide box or two, you can control where the snakes are in their cage. In this type of setup, you need only to lift the hide box to see the milksnake.

Fresh water in a low but fairly large dish is mandatory. Milksnakes will often soak in their water for a day or two at a time, especially when entering the shedding cycle. Most of these snakes require a fairly high relative humidity in their cage to shed properly. An alternative to this can be provided by supplying a covered plastic shoebox of barely dampened, unmilled sphagnum moss in which they may hide and keep their skin soft and pliable.

Subspecies: As mentioned earlier, there are simply too many subspecies of milksnake to discuss individually. However, we will discuss two popular races found in the United States.

The first is the **Scarlet kingsnake,** *L. t. elapsoides*. This is a subspecies of the southeastern United States and is considered a coral snake mimic.

Coloration: In the United States it is easy to differentiate between the scarlet kingsnake and the coral snake. The coral snake has the two caution colors, red and yellow, abutting one another. The scarlet kingsnake has the two caution colors separated by a band of black. The eastern coral snake also has a black nose, whereas the scarlet king is mainly red.

The scarlet kingsnake, Lampropeltis triangulum elapsoides, *is a very secretive snake of the southeastern United States.*

The scarlet kingsnake is easily recognized due to its red snout, narrow, supple torso, and 12–22 red bands. Neither the red nor the yellow (or white) scales have black tipping. It is usually active at night or at dusk on overcast, rainy evenings. This snake averages 20 inches (51 cm) in total length.

In the wild, scarlet kingsnakes consume lizards and smaller snakes. The

Although not mentioned specifically in our text, the broad, clean, red bands, large size, and ready availability of captive bred specimens combine to make the Sinaloan milksnake, Lampropeltis tria sinaloae, *a hobbyist favorite.*

The Mexican milksnake, Lampropeltis triangulum annulatus, *ranges from central Texas southward through much of northeastern Mexico. Bright when young, the colors tend to darken with advancing age.*

about 30 inches in total length, but may occasionally exceed a rather heavy-bodied 40 inches. Its larger size allows a greater diversity of diet. Adults readily consume lizards, other snakes, and rodents. The neonates, 8–9 inches at hatching, can consume pinky mice.

Mexican milksnakes are vividly ringed in red, black, and yellow (or white) but have a predominantly black belly and usually a black nose. They are found from central Texas southward into eastern Mexico.

Gray-banded Kingsnake, *L. alterna* ssp.

The gray-banded kingsnake is considered a prize species by many milksnake and kingsnake collectors. A moderate-sized species—adults attain a total length of about 4 feet.

Coloration: This species is the most variably colored of the kingsnakes found in the United States. The two color extremes of this snake are so distinctly different that they were long thought to be two full species. One phase, initially called the Davis Mountain kingsnake, was described in 1901 as *L. alterna*. The second of the color phases was first described in 1950 as a separate (and very rare) species, the Blair's kingsnake (*L. blairi*).

When, in 1970, it was found that both alterna and blairi can hatch from a single clutch of eggs, the name *L. blairi* became invalid.

The "alterna phase" derives its name from the white-edged dark bands that encircle the snake's olive-gray to gray body. Along the torso, these alternate—one is entire and the next is broken. The neck and tail are often patterned with blotches rather than bands. The alterna phase may or may not have red or orange present in the center of the complete bands. If red is present, it is on the neck or tail.

kingsnake will also consume newly born mice. As captives, many wild-collected specimens retain their preference for lizard prey, particularly favoring small skinks. Captive hatchlings that steadfastly refuse other prey may accept baby skinks or tail sections from larger skinks.

The **Mexican milksnake** (*L. t. annulata*) is larger. As an adult, it is

A lizard-eater by nature, gray-banded kingsnakes, Lampropeltis alterna, *are not always easily acclimated to a diet of lab rodents.*

It is the "Blair's phase" of the gray-banded kingsnake that is most variable. Some specimens are very brilliantly colored, their white-edged black saddles containing broad areas of brilliant red or orange. Other specimens may be very dark and become even more dark with advancing age. The red may be difficult to discern on older specimens.

Either phase may predominate in any given section of the species range. Within the United States, the gray-banded kingsnake occurs in southwest Texas; a few specimens have been found in immediately adjacent Eddy County, New Mexico. The snake also occurs well southward in north central Mexico.

Reptile breeders across the country now offer hatchlings every year. Prices vary according to attractiveness, with the most brilliant or "classic" specimens being the most expensive. All tame and feed readily.

In nature, gray-banded kingsnakes prey primarily on lizards. Hatchlings are especially dependent on lizards. Even some captive-born baby specimens prefer lizards to mice.

Sonoran Mountain Kingsnake, *L. pyromelana* ssp.

Most people who are lucky enough to see this beautiful tri-colored snake in the wild are impressed at how cryptic the bright bands of red, black and white are in nature.

Sonoran Mountain kingsnakes are found in high elevations of 3,000–9,000 feet in pine, fir, and oak forests. Juniper and chaparral and numerous herbs form a sparse to heavy undercover.

The five subspecies, some of which are questionable, are defined by their markings (ring and scale counts) and by their site of origin. The expanses of desert lowland between the mountain ranges prevent crossover of

Some gray-banded kingsnakes are quite dark in color and become more so with advancing age.

specimens and ensure the integrity of the races.

Sonoran Mountain kingsnakes are much in demand by hobbyists because they are remarkably beautiful creatures which retain their brilliance and contrast throughout their life. All are clad in rings of brilliant red, jet black, and white. Each race seems

Sonoran Mountain kingsnakes, Lampropeltis pyromelana *ssp., are among the most beautifully colored of all tricolors. This intergrade specimen is of confused lineage.*

more attractive than the next. The only of the four subspecies that is not found in the United States is *L. p. knoblochi*, the beautiful Chihuahua Mountain king.

Sonoran Mountain kingsnakes are easily maintained, but do require brumation (=hibernation) to breed successfully. However, if merely kept as a pet, the winter cooling is not required.

Caution: Wild kingsnakes (of all kinds) that prey heavily on amphibians are likely to have many endoparasites. Wild-collected kingsnakes should be watched carefully for signs of parasitism. Your veterinarian can use a stool sample to diagnose whether a problem exists.

Bullsnakes, Gopher Snakes, and Pine Snakes, Genus *Pituophis*

Despite their different appearances and belonging to different genera, the big constricting snakes of *Pituophis* are very closely allied to both the kingsnake and the rat snake. Occasional hybrids between gopher and rat snakes have been found in the wild, and hobbyists have produced similar hybrids.

In conformation, *Pituophis* are heavy bodied and small headed. All are capable of powerful constriction but may simply swallow small prey items alive. Because of a projection on the glottis, the bull, pine, and gopher snakes can hiss loudly. The scales are prominently keeled. They tend to be aggressive at first but can be tamed with handling.

All members of the genus *Pituophis* have an enlarged rostral (nose tip) scale to assist in burrowing, a habit best displayed by the very secretive eastern pine snakes.

Habitats: These snakes are inhabitants of arid and semiarid areas, plains, prairies, and sandhills. Even in the southeast where rain is plentiful, the pine snakes are associated with areas of sharp moisture runoff and well-drained soils.

Habits: Of principally diurnal (daytime) habits during periods of moderate temperature, these snakes may also be active at night during periods of hot weather. This is especially true of bull and gopher snakes.

Although large specimens of the gopher, bull, and pine snakes that are accustomed to wild prey may be reluctant to accept laboratory mice and rats, this reluctance is seldom seen in hatchlings taken from the wild. As a matter of fact, babies of all usually prove voracious feeders and fast growers. These snakes are all large as hatchlings, and most can easily accept a somewhat less than half-grown mouse as their initial meal.

When encountered in the field, the snakes of this genus can prove nervous and irritable. Many will vibrate their tail strenuously and, if the snake is amid dead vegetation, the noise sounds like the "whirr" of a rattlesnake. The gopher, bull, and pine snakes are also top contenders with the wolf for championship in the "Three Little Pigs" contest—these snakes "huff and puff," (the noise sounds like a steam leak!), loop into a striking "S," and do everything possible to appear formidable. In most cases, they succeed. We would be very reluctant to reach for an irritated 6-foot pine snake. These snakes are not all bluff.

Although these snakes are capable of burrowing, the pine snakes do so extensively.

Baby *Pituophis* tame quickly, but if repeatedly and gently handled even wild adults will become fairly tame. However, be aware for that one day your snake hisses and coils when you approach its cage, use caution. Gently lifting your snake first on a snakehook, then transferring it to your hand will often quiet it.

Bullsnake, *P. catenifer sayi*

Coloration: Like many of the snakes in this genus, the dorsal blotches of the bullsnake are usually darker anteriorly and posteriorly than at midbody. Blotch count is usually 41 or more. The blotches on the tail appear more like rings than saddles. Although the ground color of the bullsnake may vary according to the substrate on which it is found, this is often a warm yellow or yellow-tan at midbody.

In the last few years, several color morphs of the bullsnake have been developed. Among these are chalk white (axanthic), with incomplete or obscured charcoal dorsal markings, albinos, snow, ghost, and hypomelanistic phases.

Size: With a record size of 8.33 feet, the bullsnake is one of the largest snakes in North America. The adults are of impressively heavy girth.

Range: The bullsnake is the easternmost representative of this species. It ranges widely throughout the North American plains states, from southern Alberta, Canada to well south of the U.S. border in northeastern Mexico.

Until recently the bullsnake, and the more westerly gopher snakes, were considered subspecies of the pine snake, *P. melanoleucus.*

Additional subspecies: Besides the bullsnake, there are approximately ten additional races of gopher snake, *P. catenifer* ssp. Gopher snakes are widely distributed over much of western North America from southern British Columbia and Saskatchewan southward to central mainland Mexico, all of the Baja Peninsula and many of the islands.

Of the various gopher snakes, six are now commonly represented in herpetocultural projects. These include: the Great Basin, the Pacific, the Sonoran, the San Diegan, the Central Baja, and the Cape gopher snakes.

These six are all mainland and Baja forms. They are all being captive bred in fair numbers.

The **Great Basin Gopher Snake** (*P. c. deserticola*) is the northernmost and one of the darker subspecies of gopher snakes. The dorsal blotches of this inland race are black and often interconnect with the lateral blotches. Although snakes of 6 feet in length have been reported, 4.5–5 feet in length is normal. The range of the Great Basin gopher snake includes southcentral British Columbia (Canada) southward to southeastern California, northern Arizona, and extreme northwestern New Mexico.

The **Pacific Gopher Snake** (*P. c. catenifer*) is perhaps the most variable race. It occurs naturally in both blotched and striped morphs, and albino specimens of both have also been found. The availability and colorations of albinos have been artificially enhanced by captive-breeding projects.

Hatchlings are *much* paler than the adults. The Pacific gopher snake is usually seen in adult lengths of about

The Pacific gopher snake, Pituophis catenifer catenifer, *an albino pictured here, is a popular pet trade snake.*

Many examples of the Pacific gopher snake are striped rather than blotched.

4.5–5 feet. The range of this subspecies includes much of western Oregon and California.

The **San Diegan Gopher Snake** (*P. c. annectens*) occasionally exceeds 6 feet in length, but is more commonly 4–5 feet. This race also has an albino form, but most now available, are the result of a long ago intergrading of a normal San Diegan gopher snake with an albino Pacific. The San Diegan gopher snake is found from central California (Santa Barbara county) southward to central Baja California Norte. Although this snake seems most common in coastal areas, it is commonly found in mountains and desert regions.

The **Sonoran Gopher Snake** (*P. c. affinis*) is one of the most attractive and most commonly seen of the gopher snakes. The naturally occurring albinos have strawberry red saddles on a pearl white to pale pinky-white ground color. The Sonoran gopher snake is commonly seen from southern Colorado southward through most of Arizona, New Mexico, and western Texas. The range then continues well southward onto the Mexican mainland. Most specimens are adult at from 4.5–5 feet.

The range of the **Central Baja Gopher Snake** (*P. c. bimaris*) is described by its common name. Adult size is 4.5 to rarely 6 feet. Albinos and other color morphs have now been developed.

The **Cape Gopher Snake** (*P. c. vertebralis*) ranges from La Paz, Baja California Sur, southward to the tip of the peninsula. This is the most brilliantly colored of the gopher snakes. The ground color is tannish-orange to buff anteriolaterally, lighter yellow posteriolaterally, rich orange on the anterior dorsum and somewhat lighter posteriorly. The head is often a rich, unmarked, orange on the crown. This fades to light tan on the chin. Understandably, this is one of the most coveted of the gopher snakes, and hatchlings consistently command high prices. As with many of the members of this genus, the hatchlings and juveniles are paler than the adults. In many cases the pallid coloration of a newly hatched specimen will give little

Gopher snakes are now bred both in normal and albino forms as well as with varying patterns. This is a normally colored Sonoran gopher snake, Pituophis catenifer affinis.

indication of the color and beauty it will assume as an adult. Both albino and "patternless" Cape gopher snake have now been developed. Adult size is 4 feet, although some may reach 5.5 feet.

Pine Snakes, *P. melanoleucus* ssp.

The four races of pine snake vary widely in color by subspecies, but to a lesser degree, within a subspecies. As with the bull and gopher snakes, herpetoculturists have increased this variation by developing or enhancing both ground color and pattern intensity.

The **Northern Pine Snake** (*P. m. melanoleucus*) is impressively large and often equally impressively belligerent. It has a curiously disjunct distribution from the Pine Barrens of New Jersey to central Kentucky in the north to central South Carolina and southern Alabama in the south. However, within this vast area the northern pine snake is found only in a few tiny pockets of habitat.

It is this race, perhaps more than any other, about which hobbyists think

The Cape gopher snake, Pituophis (catenifer) vertebralis, *of the southern Baja Peninsula, is one of the most brightly colored members of the entire genus.*

when the generic term of pine snake is mentioned. Northern pines have long been coveted for their highly contrasting pattern. The ground coloration of most northern pine snakes is chalk white. However, buffs and reds are

Albinism is well established in nearly all members of the bull, pine, and gopher snakes. Pictured is an albino northern pine snake.

Northern pine snakes, Pituophis melanoleucus melanoleucus, are large, powerful constrictors of sandy habitats that burrow readily. This is a red-phase juvenile.

89

The black pine snake, Pituophis melanoleucus lodingi, *is the darkest race of this eastern group. Once considered rare, captive breeding programs have now assured its ready availability.*

sometimes seen. The latter color has now been enhanced by herpetoculturists who now sell "red phase northern pines." The greatest authenticated length for this race is 83 inches.

Louisiana Pine Snake (*P. m. ruthveni*) is the only pine snake found west of the Mississippi River. It is also the most uncommon and poorly known of the pine snakes. It is found primarily in central western Louisiana and adjacent eastern central Texas, but at no point is its known range contiguous with that of the bullsnake.

This resident of pine flatwoods and dunes is marginally the smallest of the pine snakes, with the known record size being just 70.25 inches.

It is only recently that the Louisiana pine snake has become available to private herpetoculturists. Although captive-breeding programs are making this snake more readily available, it still remains more expensive than most others. Because of its comparative rarity, there seems to have been little effort by herpetoculturists to breed for albinism or other anomalies.

Until recently, the **Black Pine Snake** (*P. m. lodingi*) was considered an expensive rarity by herpetoculturists. The success of captive-breeding programs has changed this though. In fact, the black pine snake is now available to anyone who wants one.

Like many other dark snakes (kingsnakes and rat snakes), the degree of patterning visible on black pine snakes varies. Hatchlings tend to show more patterning than adults. Black pine snakes have been seen rarely in Washington Parish, Louisiana and Escambia County, Florida.

It is perhaps because they are colored so very differently from the other subspecies of pine snakes that black pines are eagerly sought by hobbyists and breeders. The darkest snakes are the most in demand. Of all the many subspecies in this genus, the black pine is the only race to be so heavily pigmented with melanin.

Like the other races of pine snakes, black pines, which reach 76 inches in length, are affiliated with sandy pineland habitats.

The **Florida Pine Snake** (*P. m. mugitus*) might be more appropriately called the "southeastern" pine snake; its range includes eastern Georgia, southeastern South Carolina, and all but southernmost Florida. The ground color of hatchlings may be suffused with pink, peach, or pale-orange. Albinos and other color phases of this race have been developed.

Although they seem to be more secretive than rare, the Florida pine snake is a regulated species in Florida. With a confirmed record length of 90 inches, this is the largest of the pine snakes.

Mexican Bullsnake, *P. deppei* ssp.

Once uncommon in herpetoculture, breeding programs are making the Mexican bullsnake a readily available snake. As with all snakes with which demand exceeds supply, the price of Mexican bullsnakes remains rather high. *P. d. deppei*, the more westerly race, is a snake of the Sierran elevations in central northern Mexico. It is the more prominently blotched of the two races, having rather precisely outlined charcoal to chocolate dorsal blotches against a ground color which may vary from gold to orange. Hatchlings are less brilliantly colored than adults.

The more easterly of the two races of Mexican bullsnake (*P. d. janni*) is found in the Mexican states of Coahuila, Nuevo Leon, Hidalgo, and Tamaulipas. It is pallid as a juvenile with even the better defined anterior blotches appearing faded. The sandy tan ground color of the juveniles (which may have an orangish wash) intensifies with age. The ground color of the adult is golden to a rather bright orange and is most intense at mid-body. With age, the dorsal blotches *may* become somewhat better defined.

Both races are known to exceed 5.5 feet in total length.

Caging: Although young gopher snakes, bullsnakes, and pine snakes can be kept in plastic breeding trays, the large adults need sizable cages. We believe that a pair makes an ideal display when kept in a 75-gallon (or larger) naturalistic terrarium.

Breeding: These snakes are now regularly bred in captivity. The methods for cycling the pine, bull, and gopher snakes reproductively are similar to those used to cycle rat and kingsnakes (see pages 26–27 for guidelines).

Although the clutches are relatively small, the eggs and hatchlings of all of these snakes are large. Hatchlings of the Great Basin gopher snake may be 12–14 inches in total length and those of the bull and Sonoran gopher snake may near 19 inches in length. In cap-

tivity, the largest clutches, largest eggs, and healthiest babies are obtained from the best-fed and healthiest females.

Incubation techniques for the eggs of these snakes is similar to that used for the eggs of the king and rat snakes (see pp. 28–30).

Both races of the Mexican bullsnake are hardy and attractive. Pictured are Pituophis deppei jani, *top, and* P. d. deppei, *bottom.*

The red color phase of the African brown house snake, Lamprophis fuliginosus, *pictured here, is becoming popular with American hobbyists.*

Brown House Snake, *Lamprophis fuliginosus*

Although the African genus *Lamprophis* contains several species, the only one to be firmly established in U.S. herpetoculture is *L. fuliginosus*, the brown house snake. It is small enough

It is not yet known with certainty whether piebald characteristics, such as shown on this brown house snake, are genetically influenced or induced by incubating conditions.

to be conveniently housed and is hardy.

Coloration and appearance: The brown house snake has a variety of pleasing natural colors—not all of them brown. Black specimens are often found, as are olive ones. The colors most in demand in U.S. herpetoculture are terracotta (called red by hobbyists) and golden brown. A pretty, warm chocolate phase is also favored. The venter may be pale yellow to opalescent. There are two narrow stripes on each side of the head. The upper one runs from the tip of the snout and extends back to the neck. The second stripe runs diagonally from the rear of the eye to the angle of the jaw. Amelanistic specimens are known. The cat-like eyes of this snake are large, and the head is quite distinct from the neck. House snakes are crepuscular and nocturnal.

Size: As adults, brown house snakes can reach 2–3.5 feet. Hatchlings measure between 8 and 10 inches in length and usually accept pinky mice readily.

Range: The brown house snake is a habitat generalist, but seems especially prevalent in open grasslands. As indicated by its common name, it is a well-known species near human dwellings. It occurs throughout most of subsaharan Africa.

Breeding: The largest, healthiest female brown house snakes produce up to 15 eggs per clutch, and several clutches may be laid annually at 4–6-week intervals. To cycle, these fecund snakes require only a slight winter cooling. Although we maintained them with a natural photoperiod, this does not seem as important as with certain other snake species. Eggs incubate for about 2 months at 82°F.

Caging: Newly captured brown house snakes are prone to bite. However, they acclimate and quiet rather quickly. These are not overly active snakes. A young pair can be easily maintained in a 15-gallon terrarium. This has a floor space of 12 × 24 inches and a height of 12 inches. The cage should be provided with several secure hiding areas, a small, untippable water dish, and an easily cleaned substrate. A summer temperature of 78–86°F seems acceptable. During the daytime, we provide a basking area of about 90°F. Only gravid females use this basking area with any regularity.

Comments: We believe that brown house snakes are one of the best of the readily available pet trade species. As the more colorful strains become steadily available, these snakes will become more popular.

Rough Green Snake, *Opheodrys aestivus*

If you are squeamish about feeding traditional prey items to a snake, but still have an interest in snakes, the insectivorous rough green snake is a species you should consider. Throughout its life, the rough green snake is an insectivore. In the wild it eats a variety of insects, but particularly likes nonhairy caterpillars. In captivity it will eat vitamin-mineral dusted, gut-loaded crickets (crickets fed a vitamin and mineral enhanced diet before being offered as food), as well as other nonnoxious insects.

Coloration: This little snake has a rather standardized leaf-green dorsally, but may vary from white to butter yellow or yellowish-green ventrally. Hatchlings are much duller than the adults. The scales are keeled, hence the "rough" in its common name.

Size: Although some snakes have measured more than 3.5 feet in total length, the usual size is between 2 and 3 feet.

Range: The rough (formerly, keeled) green snake may be found from southern New Jersey and east-

The elliptical pupil of the brown house snake is contracted during the day and widely dilated at night.

ern Kansas southward to the Gulf Coast. It is also found in northeastern Mexico.

Breeding: Breeding rough green snakes may take little (for southern specimens) to considerable (for northern specimens) preparation. Southern specimens usually need only a slight

The rough green snake, Opheodrys aestivus, *is a small insectivore that is offered in the pet trade with increasing frequency.*

winter cooling, lowered relative humidity, and lessened photoperiod to cycle. Examples from more northerly areas will require a 90-day period of full hibernation.

Green snakes breed when the lengthening days of spring begin elevating temperatures and humidity increases. Healthy, well-acclimated rough green snakes may double clutch each year. The clutch size is quite small (1–10 eggs often 3–6), and the eggs are noticeably elongate. Depending on temperature, humidity, and genetics, the incubation duration may vary from about 4 weeks to 9 weeks or more. Hatchlings are a slender 7.5 inches at emergence.

Caging: This snake does well in a terrarium setup with small frogs, salamanders, or lizards. Instead of worrying whether the snake will eat its cagemates, you should worry about the cagemates eating the snake. This dainty and diminutive racer relative is persistently arboreal and very active in nature. We suggest that captives be housed in a vertically oriented cage with growing, vining plants such as philodendron or pothos. The plants offer these little snakes the seclusion and security they seek and help keep the cages humid as well. Rough green snakes will often not drink from a dish of standing water, preferring instead to drink droplets of misted water hanging from branches, leaves, terrarium sides, or from their own bodies. Many will use a water dish if the water is roiled with an aquarium air stone. We suggest a terrarium with a floor space of no less than 18 × 36 inches and prefer those with a height of 30 or more inches. We also suggest that full-spectrum lighting and vitamin and mineral-enhanced foods be provided. These little snakes will dehydrate quickly. A suitable regimen of providing water (probably misting) must be used daily.

Although most rough green snakes currently offered in the U.S. pet trade are wild collected, hobbyists are now beginning to breed the species.

The "Odd-Toothed" Snakes

Eastern Hog-Nosed Snake, *Heterodon platirhinos*

The genus *Heterodon* contains three species. Although the western species eats a greater variety of food than either eastern species, all feed preferentially on toads. All three are characterized by upturned, enlarged rostral scales—a feature which gives them "hog" noses. The noses of both the southern and the western hognoses (*H. simus* and *H. nasicus*, respectively) are sharply upturned. The snout of the eastern hog-nosed snake, *H. platirhinos*, is the least accentuated.

Hog-nosed snakes are less feared by most people than other snakes. Many people just seem to *like* hognoses. Perhaps it is because hognose snakes move more slowly than many other snakes, or maybe it is

Many examples of the eastern hog-nosed snake, Heterodon platirhinos, *are less colorful than this calico specimen.*

their inherent pudginess or repertoire of defensive ploys that endears them.

The snake's defense strategies include striking at a tormentor with a closed mouth, spreading the head and neck in a fearsome "cobralike" display, and "playing possum."

Playing possum is usually the last rite in the defensive sequence. The threatened snake will suddenly begin writhing to and fro, mouth open, tongue lolling. It will appear to be in extreme agony. Suddenly the hog-nosed snake will roll over, belly up, then become quiet and limp—to all appearances, dead. During this last stage a hog-nosed snake will show no signs of life, unless it is turned right-side up. Then, quick as a wink it will roll over again. It seems as if the snake thinks that the only way to impersonate a dead snake is to lie belly up.

Caution: Some people who have been bitten by hog-nosed snakes have experienced symptoms of mild envenomation. Localized mild to severe swelling and redness have occurred. Although hog-nosed snakes seldom if ever purposely bite, care should be exercised when handling these snakes. The toxic saliva is probably a mechanism for quickly disabling prey and does not seem to have been developed for defensive purposes.

Coloration: The eastern hog-nosed snake is a variably colored species. Examples may vary from straw yellow between the dark dorsal blotches (darker laterally and brightest anterovertebrally), to olive to nearly a jet black. Some areas may have one phase or the other, whereas other areas may have all of the color schemes. Hatchlings are paler than adults. Albinos and hypomelanistic specimens have been found.

Size: Although hog-nosed snakes of more than 2.5 feet in length are seldom encountered, specimens of more

A normally colored and an albino southern hog-nosed snake, Heterodon simus, *in the breeding programs of Hogwild provide an interesting contrast in color.*

than 3.5 feet in length have been recorded.

Range: Eastern hog-nosed snakes range widely over most of the eastern half of the United States and in extreme southeastern Canada.

Caging: Because none are overly active, hog-nosed snakes seem content in fairly small cages. Many hobbyists keep them in plastic sweater boxes. Because we enjoy naturalistic terraria more than stark cages, we usually provide our hog-nosed snakes with a thick substrate of sand. We also often place a clump or two of "bunch" or "field" grass in the cage. Its attractiveness, and the cover it provides the snakes, persist long after the grass has died. Rocks are also provided, as long as they can't settle on the snakes if they burrow beneath them. Fresh water is always available.

Comments: Hog-nosed snakes, collectively, are very adept at both burrowing and rooting out buried toads (a main component of their diets). In both pursuits, the hognoses' keeled and upturned rostral scales serve them well. Hog-nosed snakes are members of the grouping of colubrines known as the xenodontines—the "odd-toothed" snakes. In the case of the hognoses, the reference is to large teeth—the "toad stickers"—at the rear of the upper jaws. Toads, when confronted or when grasped by a snake, immediately inflate their bodies with air in an effort to make themselves unswallowable. This ploy works with many snakes, but usually fails with hog-nosed snakes which merely use their large teeth at the rear of the jaw to penetrate and deflate the body of the toad.

Should your hog-nosed snake be fed mice? Some hobbyists and breeders advocate feeding mice to hog-nosed snakes. Although mice are a natural component of the diet of the western hog-nosed snake, they are less natural to either the eastern or the southern species. All can be acclimated to take mice, initially by scenting a mouse with a toad. Some eastern and southern hog-nosed snakes may even accept mice volun-

tarily. However, the long-term effects of such an unnatural diet have not yet been determined. Such a comparatively high-fat and difficult to digest prey item may affect lifespan and reproductive potential. Many hog-nosed snakes have died soon after eating live or freshly killed mice. Fewer deaths have been attributed to hog-nosed snakes that have ingested thawed, once-frozen mice. We believe that the feeding of mice to eastern and southern hog-nosed snakes should be approached with caution and the results monitored closely.

Other species: The southern and the western hog-nosed snakes are of quite similar appearance. Of the two, the southern is somewhat more brilliantly colored. The dark orbital bridle of the **southern hog-nosed snake** (*H. simus*) is usually much less well developed than on either the eastern or the western hog-nosed snake. The southern hog-nosed snake has about 25 dark dorsal blotches and often some pale orange or even peach coloring vertebrally. The colors tend to be brightest anteriorly. The sides are duskier.

The range of the southern hog-nosed snake includes a wide swath along the Atlantic Coastal Plain from central North Carolina to Gulf Coast central Mississippi (the Louisiana-Mississippi state line). As mentioned earlier, the southern hognose is also found southward in Florida to the region of Tampa Bay on Florida's west coast to Okeechobee County on the east.

The southern hog-nosed snake reaches a maximum of 2 feet in length.

Because toads are the favored food of the southern hog-nosed snake, few specimens have fed voluntarily on small pinkys.

The **western hog-nosed snake** (*H. nasicus*) has three very similar

Because of their varied diet, the various subspecies of the western hog-nosed snake are the easiest of the three species to keep in captivity. A Plains hog-nosed snake, Heterodon nasicus nasicus *is pictured here.*

appearing subspecies. These are *H. n. gloydi*, the dusty hog-nosed snake of disjunct distribution along the extreme eastern part of the range (Texas, Oklahoma, Kansas), the Plains hog-nosed snake (*H. n. nasicus*) of the northern parts of the range (northern Texas and eastern New Mexico northward) and the Mexican hognose (*H. n. kennerlyi*); (southern Texas southward). To identify the subspecies, we refer you to *Conant and Collins Field Guide to the Reptiles and Amphibians of the Eastern and Central United States.*

The range of the western hog-nosed snake (not differentiating for subspecies) extends southward through the Plains states from extreme southern Saskatchewan and southeastern Alberta Canada to far south into eastern Mexico.

Western hog-nosed snakes reach a length of just under 40 inches.

Of the three species of hog-nosed snakes, only the westerns routinely include rodents in their diet. Because of this, they are rapidly gaining the favor of herpetoculturists.

Neotropical Indigo Snakes, the Cribos, *Drymarchon corais* ssp.

Despite being big, messy, often short-tempered, heavily parasitized and only marginally pretty, cribos remain popular with many hobbyists. These are wide-ranging, very active habitat generalists which are related to the indigo snakes.

The **eastern indigo snake** (*D. c. couperi*) is a federally endangered species that can neither be collected nor sold in interstate commerce in the United States, even if legally held and bred, without an appropriate permit. There are numerous hobbyists breeding the race. Before being regulated, this snake was one of the most eagerly sought by reptile collectors.

Of the several races of neotropical indigo snake, the yellow-tailed cribo, Drymarchon corais corais, *is the most colorful.*

Although the **Texas indigo** (*D. c. erebennus*) is not considered endangered, it is a protected species both in Texas and in Mexico. It cannot be legally collected without a permit.

The **yellow-tailed cribo,** *Drymarchon corais corais* is the most brightly colored of the group.

Black-tailed cribo, *D. c. melanurus*

Coloration: The amount of black coloration on the posterior of the black-tailed cribo can vary tremendously. Some specimens may lack most of the black pigmentation; others may be black from tip of the tail to a point well anterior of midbody. In all cases, dark markings radiate downward from the eye to the lip, a vertical dark slash is at the rear of the jaw, and a heavy diagonal black slash is on each side of the neck.

The scales of the anterior of the body and head are olive-yellow to olive-tan. Healthy adults can be heavy bodied, but because of an almost invariable abundance of parasites, wild adults are very thin, with prominent backbones. Hatchlings look like diminutives of the adults, but are proportionately more slender.

Size: Although not the longest subspecies, the black-tailed cribo often exceeds 7 feet in length and may be as much as 10 feet.

Range: The black-tailed cribo is found throughout much of Central America. It is an adept climber, is fast on the ground, and is capable of swimming if necessary. Black-tailed cribos are found in forest openings, natural savanna edges, and manmade clearings.

Breeding: Cribos and indigo snakes have moderate clutches of large eggs. Hatchlings can vary between 16 and 24 inches in total length. At hatching, the babies are well able to eat small mice, frogs, and other small prey.

In keeping with their tropical habitat, these cribos can be cycled reproductively with just a moderate winter cooling combined with a lowered relative humidity and a reduced photoperiod. This cycling should last for 45–65 days. Cribos will often breed during, or even at the advent of this period. This is in keeping with eastern indigos which are such effective thermoregulators that they can keep active in all but the very coldest weather and breed during the winter months. Sperm may be held for several months prior to fertilizing the eggs.

Black-tailed cribos may lay at any time of the spring or early summer (no cribo/indigo has double clutched at our facility), and incubation can take from 2 months to more than 2.5 months.

It seems that cribos fed a varied diet of birds, mammals, and amphibians breed more readily than those fed only rodents.

Caging: Cribos are big snakes that, in nature, are immensely active "search and overpower" predators.

As would be expected from such a snake, they do best in large cages. A cage with a floor space of 4 × 8 feet would probably suffice for a pair of cribos. However, a larger cage may be better. Although limbs or elevated platforms are not mandatory, the snakes will use them if provided. A large receptacle of fresh water will be used for both drinking and soaking. The water should be frequently cleaned and sterilized to help prevent transference of endoparasites. Wild-collected cribos should be checked for endoparasites as soon as possible.

Adult cribos taken from the wild may strike savagely at movements outside of their cage. Nose injuries can occur from such actions. It may be necessary to tape opaque paper or cloth to the front of the glass until the snakes become less agitated.

Although it takes a dedicated person to keep a cribo, with proper care, persistent gentle handling, and slow keeper movements, these snakes will usually quiet down and thrive.

Photography

We consider photography an enjoyable way to "keep" snakes or to record their behavior. Because we seldom take snakes from the wild anymore, our photographs help us remember and enjoy moments and specimens which would otherwise soon lose their mystique and, through our slide presentations, we can share the enjoyment with other enthusiasts.

In the past 6 years or so, with the expansion of the business of ecotourism, it is much easier to see snakes for yourself. Firms, such as Green Tracks, Inc. (Berkeley, CA), specialize in reptile and amphibian sighting and photography trips. Green Tracks regularly guides small groups to many regions in Latin America where the tour participants may see boas and other equally interesting reptiles and amphibians. In case you prefer to stay closer to home, zoos now offer naturalistic displays of snakes—an inexpensive way for you to practice your photography skills.

Although you have a wide choice of film types, from stills to videos to digital formats, we prefer slides because they adapt well to our presentations.

"Capturing" snakes on film at home or in the wild requires discipline, skill, a little knowledge, and luck. When developed, each photo will help you see how to "shoot" the next photograph better.

The equipment required will depend on several variables, including the sizes of the snakes you hope to photograph, whether the photos will be of captives, staged, or in the wild and whether or not you are willing to devote the time necessary to be successful. Of course, photographing captive snakes is much easier than pursuing and photographing the animals in the wild.

Basic Equipment Needs

A sturdy 35-mm camera body with interchangeable lenses is suggested. You don't necessarily need a new camera body and lenses; we've used quality second-hand equipment for many of our photographic ventures. You do need a photo supply dealer who can advise about the condition of the equipment you're buying and who can tell you about some features of that particular lens or body. (Second-hand camera equipment only rarely comes with manuals of any sort, and operating by guess when presented with a once-in-a-lifetime photo opportunity is not comforting.)

A 35mm camera and lenses can be fairly inexpensive if purchased secondhand.

Lenses: The lenses we use include:

- 28-mm wide angle for habitat photos
- 50-mm standard for habitat photos
- 100-mm macro for closeups (suitable for almost every purpose)
- 75–205-mm zoom lens for variable fieldwork
- 400-mm fixed focal length telephoto lens for fieldwork
- 120–600 zoom lens for distant but variable fieldwork

Different lenses will be needed for different applications.

Strobes: A series of dedicated strobes (a dedicated strobe interfaces with the camera f-stop setting to furnish appropriate light levels)

Lens adapter: A 1.25× to 2× power lens adapter (doubler).

Film: ISO 50 slide film is slower, hence less "grainy" than the faster films often used for other purposes. This slower film will give you the best results, but also requires a bright day or electronic flashes to compensate for the slow speed. The higher the ISO, the less light you will need to photograph, but your pictures will be "grainier." If you are taking pictures in hopes of publishing them, use ISO 50 slide film. If you are taking photos for your own enjoyment, use either slide or print film, as you prefer.

Tripod: A sturdy tripod (an absolute necessity for the telephoto lenses) will keep your camera steady while you take that "once-in-a-lifetime" shot. Camera equipment with lenses is heavy, especially if you're out in the field and have walked through waist-deep water and then scaled a couple of hillsides. The equipment is heavy even if you're indoors. Having a strong friend to help is recommended.

Camera body: Always have at least one spare camera body available.

Some Photographic Hints

For staged photography, create a small suitably natural setting by using a sand or leaf substrate with additional props of rocks or limbs—whatever is most appropriate for the species you're photographing—on a stage. We use a small lazy Susan as a stage, enabling us to rotate the stage with the animal on it, for

A simple photography stage can be made from a plastic trash can and a lazy Susan.

different photographic angles. This works, providing that you move very slowly, both in your own actions and in rotating the stage. If you don't have a lazy Susan, just arrange the setting items on a tabletop or on a tree stump (outdoors or indoors, depending on where you are at the time), put the snake in place and (if you're very lucky) focus and shoot. Having another person standing by to catch or reposition the snake will help.

Often, if you frighten the snake, it will pause long enough in place to permit you to get a few shots.

We created a backing for our stage with the top half of a round trash or garbage can, sectioned to size and then bolted into place just inside the edge rim of the lazy Susan. Black velvet clipped around the inside surface of the background is a good background for reptile shots.

If you're striving for field photographs, approach the animal slowly and obliquely. Avoid eye contact. If

Use a tripod to avoid blurred shots.

the snake notices you (most will!), freeze for a moment, then begin moving again. Above all, keep trying. Don't get discouraged. We always try to quickly take a photo or two, regardless of how bad the setting, then strive with each encounter with the species or subspecies, to improve the quality.

(above) *It is the gray-banded kingsnakes,* Lampropeltis alterna, *with the greatest pattern contrasts and brightest colors (such as this one) that are most in demand by hobbyists.*

(right) *Brazilian rainbow boas,* Epicrates cenchria cenchria, *are very pretty, rather large, and reasonably hardy snakes that begin breeding rather late in life. They are capable of considerable color changes.*

Although babies may be "snappy" most common boas quickly become accustomed to gentle handling. The phase shown here (Boa constrictor constrictor) is usually referred to as a red-tailed boa.

Small and hardy, the African house snake, Lamprophis fuliginosus, *is a powerful constrictor that is now gaining in popularity with American hobbyists.*

(above) The beautiful Mexican milksnake, Lampropeltis triangulum annulata, *ranges northward into central Texas. Once the subject of many Texas snake hunts, Mexican milksnakes are now captive bred in ever-increasing numbers.*

(above left) Mole kingsnakes, Lampropeltis calligaster rhombomaculata, *thrive when cared for as any of the common kingsnakes would be. Not all examples are as colorful as this one.*

(center left) The red-spotted garter snake, Thamnophis sirtalis concinnus *of the Pacific coast is one of the prettiest races of this wide-ranging species.*

(center bottom) Despite their high cost, green tree pythons, Morelia (Chondropython) viridis *are coveted by many advanced hobbyists.*

Useful Literature and Addresses

Affinity groups

Once obscure, herpetoculture is now a recognized hobby. In fact, many hobbyists are surprised to find how many others share their interests. Snake keepers, both casual and professional, outnumber the keepers of all other groups. Detailed additional information can be obtained from a fellow hobbyist or, in today's computer-oriented society, in any number of on-line services. You can find other enthusiasts through your local pet stores, libraries, universities, and community colleges.

Another source of information is herpetology groups. There are generalized groups of hobbyists in many large cities of the world, as well as professional societies such as the Society for the Study of Reptiles and Amphibians (SSAR).

Herpetologically Oriented Ecotours

Green Tracks
P.O. Box 9516
Berkeley, CA 94709
800-966-6539 (USA only) or
510-526-1339 world wide

Helpful Reading

Magazines (USA and England)

The below four magazines are available in many pet shops and newsstands.

Reptile & Amphibian Magazine: An excellent small-format journal that is currently produced eight times yearly. Subscriptions are available from *Reptile & Amphibian Magazine,* RD3, Box 3709-A, Pottsville, PA 17901.

Reptiles Magazine: A larger format magazine dedicated primarily to herpetoculture and conservation. *Reptiles* is a high-quality monthly publication. Subscription information may be obtained from *Reptiles Magazine,* P.O. Box 6050, Mission Viejo, CA 92690-6050.

The Vivarium: The publication of the American Federation of Herpetoculturists, *The Vivarium* is also bimonthly and of large format. As suggested by its name, *The Vivarium* is dedicated primarily to the captive care of reptiles and amphibians. It is available by membership in the AFH, P.O. Box 300067, Escondido, CA 92030-0067.

Reptilian: An English publication, *Reptilian* is dedicated primarily to the European perspective of herpetoculture and field study. This is an excellent, high-quality, monthly publication. Inquire from *The Reptilian Magazine,* 22 Firs Close, Hazlemere, High Wycombe, Bucks HP15 7TF, England.

The below listed professional journals are available only to members of the societies or, occasionally, through used book sellers.

Herpetological Review and the Journal of Herpetology: The Society for the Study of Reptiles and Amphibians is a professional level organization which publishes a nontechnical periodical, *Herp Review,* and a more

Despite being classified as a harmless species, the eastern hog-nosed snake, Heterodon platirhinos, *is one of many snakes to produce a toxic saliva. This brilliantly colored hatchling has spread its hood in a defensive display.*

scholarly journal, *Journal of Herpetology*. Subscriptions are available from SSAR, Department of Zoology, Miami University, Oxford, OH 45056.

Copeia: The American Society of Ichthyologists and Herpetologists publishes *Copeia*, a technical journal which includes reptiles, amphibians, and fish. Subscription information is available from ASIH Business Office, Dept. of Zoology, Southern Illinois University, Carbondale, IL 62901-6501.

Herpetologica: This quarterly is available through the Herpetologist's League, c/o Maureen A. Donnelly, College of Arts and Sciences, Florida International University, North Miami, FL 33181.

Glossary

Aestivation: A period of warm weather inactivity that is often triggered by excessive heat or drought.

Albino: Lacking black pigment.

Ambient temperature: The temperature of the surrounding environment.

Anerythristic: Lacking red pigment.

Anterior: Toward the front.

Anus: The external opening of the cloaca; the vent.

Arboreal: Tree dwelling.

Boid/Boidae: Boas and pythons.

Brille: The transparent "spectacle" covering the eyes of a snake.

Brumation: Often used to describe reptilian and amphibian hibernation.

Caudal: Pertaining to the tail.

cb/cb: Captive bred, captive born.

cb/ch: Captive bred, captive hatched.

Cloaca: The common chamber into which digestive, urinary, and reproductive systems empty and which itself opens exteriorly through the vent or anus.

Colubrine/Colubridae: The largest of the snake groupings, comprising such snakes as garters, rats, kings, and gophers.

Congeneric: In the same genus.

Constricting: To wrap tightly in coils and squeeze.

Convergent evolution: Evolution of two unrelated species as the result of environmental (or other) conditions.

Crepuscular: Active at dusk or dawn.

Deposition: The laying of the eggs or birthing of young.

Deposition site: The spot chosen by the female to lay her eggs or have her young.

Dimorphic: A difference in form, build, or coloration involving the same species; often sex-linked.

Diurnal: Active in the daytime.

Dorsal: Pertaining to the back; upper surface.

Dorsolateral: Pertaining to the upper sides.

Ecological niche: The precise habitat utilized by a species.

Ectothermic: "Cold-blooded."

Endothermic: "Warm-blooded."

Erythristic: A prevalence of red pigment.

Form: An identifiable species or subspecies.

Fossorial: Adapted for burrowing; a burrowing species.

Genus: A taxonomic classification of a group of species having similar characteristics. The genus is classified between the next higher designation of "family" and the next lower designation of "species." Genera is the singular of genus. It is always capitalized when written.

Glottis: The opening of the windpipe.

Gravid: The reptilian equivalent of mammalian pregnancy.

Gular: Pertaining to the throat.

Heliothermic: Pertaining to a species that basks in the sun to thermoregulate.

Hemipenes: The dual copulatory organs of male lizards and snakes.

Hemipenis: The singular form of hemipenes.

Herpetoculture: The captive breeding of reptiles and amphibians.

Herpetoculturist: One who indulges in herpetoculture.

Herpetologist: One who indulges in herpetology.

Herpetology: The study (often scientifically oriented) of reptiles and amphibians.

Hibernacula: Winter dens.

Hybrid: Offspring resulting from the breeding of two species.

Hydrate: To restore body moisture by drinking or absorption.

Insular: Island dwelling.

Intergrade: Offspring resulting from the breeding of two subspecies. Jacobson's organs: Highly enervated olfactory pits in the palate of snakes and lizards.

Juvenile: A young or immature specimen.

Keel: A ridge (along the center of a scale).

Labial: Pertaining to the lips.

Lateral: Pertaining to the side.

Melanism: A profusion of black pigment.

Middorsal: Pertaining to the middle of the back.

Midventral: Pertaining to the center of the belly or abdomen.

Monotypic: Containing but one type.

Natricine/Natricinae: A member of the subfamily containing garter water, brown, and other related colubrine snakes.

Nocturnal: Active at night.

Ontogenetic: Age-related (color) changes.

Opisthoglyphous/opisthoglyph: A colubrine snake with enlarged teeth in the rear of its upper jaw and a variably toxic saliva.

Oviparous: Reproducing by means of eggs that hatch after laying.

Ovoviviparous: Reproducing by means of shelled or membrane-contained eggs that hatch prior to, or at deposition.

Photoperiod: The daily or seasonally variable length of the hours of daylight.

Poikilothermic: A species with no internal body temperature regulation. The old term was "cold-blooded."

Postocular: To the rear of the eye.

Prey imprinting: Preferring prey of only a particular species or color.

Race: A subspecies.

Rostral: The (often modified) scale on the tip of the snout.

Rugose: Not smooth. Wrinkled or tuberculate.

Saxicolous: Rock dwelling.

Scute: Scale.

Species: A group of similar creatures that produce viable young when breeding. The taxonomic designation which falls beneath genus and above subspecies. Abbreviation: "sp."

Subspecies: The subdivision of a species. A race that may differ slightly in color, size, scalation, or other criteria. Abbreviation: "ssp."

Sympatric: Occurring together.

Taxonomy: The science of classification of plants and animals.

Terrestrial: Land dwelling.

Thermoreceptive: Sensitive to heat.

Thermoregulate: To regulate (body) temperature by choosing a warmer or cooler environment.

Thigmothermic: Pertaining to a species (often nocturnal) which thermoregulates by being in contact with a preheated surface such as a boulder or tarred road surface.

Vent: The external opening of the cloaca; the anus.

Venter: The underside of a creature; the belly.

Ventral: Pertaining to the undersurface or belly.

Ventrolateral: Pertaining to the sides of the venter (=belly).

Bibliography

Arnold, E. N., and J. A. Burton. *A Field Guide to the Reptiles and Amphibians of Britain and Europe*. London: Collins, 1978.

Bartlett, Richard D. *In Search of Reptiles and Amphibians*. Leiden: E. J. Brill, 1988.

Bartlett, Richard D. *Digest for the Successful Terrarium*. Morris Plains, NJ: TetraPress, 1989.

Bartlett, Richard D. and Patricia P. Bartlett. *Corn Snakes and Other Rat Snakes: A Complete Pet Owner's Manual*. Hauppauge, NY: Barron's, 1996.

Bartlett, Patricia P., and Ernie Wagner. *Pythons: A Complete Pet Owners Manual*. Hauppauge, NY: Barron's, 1997.

Conant, Roger, and Joseph T. Collins. *A Field Guide to Reptiles and Amphibians; Eastern and Central North America*. Boston: Houghton Mifflin Co., 1991.

Dowling, Herndon G. "A taxonomic study of the rat snakes, genus Elaphe Fitzinger. Vol. II. The subspecies of Elaphe flavirufa (Copeia)." Ann Arbor, MI: University of Michigan, 1952.

Dowling, Herndon G. "A taxonomic study of the rat snakes. Vol. VI. Validation of the genera Gonyosoma Wagler and Elaphe Fitzinger (Copeia)." Ann Arbor, MI: University of Michigan, 1958.

Markel, Ronald G., and R. D. Bartlett. *Kingsnakes and Milksnakes: A Complete Pet Owner's Manual*. Hauppauge, NY: Barron's, 1995.

Mehrtens, John M. *Living Snakes of the World in Color*. New York: Sterling Publishers, 1987.

Pope, Clifford H. *The Reptiles of China*. New York: American Museum of Natural History, 1935.

Smith, Malcolm A. *The Fauna of British India, Ceylon and Burma, Reptilia and Amphibia*. Vol. III Serpentes. London: Taylor and Francis, 1943.

Stebbins, Robert C. *A Field Guide to Western Reptiles and Amphibians*. Boston: Houghton Mifflin Co., 1985.

Staszko, Ray, and Jerry G. Walls. *Rat Snakes: A Hobbyist's Guide to Elaphe and Kin*. Neptune, NJ: TFH, 1994.

Wagner, Doug. *Boas: A Complete Pet Owner's Manual*. Hauppauge, NY: Barron's, 1996.

West, Larry, and William P. Leonard. *How to Photograph Reptiles and Amphibians*. Mechanicsburg, PA: Stackpole, 1997.

Wright, Albert H., and A. A. Wright. *Handbook of Snakes*. Vol. I. Ithaca, NY: Comstock, 1957.

Index

(**Bold** = photo)

In the past few years, the keeping and breeding of snakes has evolved from an obscure hobby to a gigantic, self-fueling industry. Before moving on to rare and difficult species, many hobbyists initially choose rat snakes, king-snakes, gopher snakes, and other species requiring a similar regimen of care. There are now so many color varieties and sub-species of these rather common snakes available that some hobbyists remain forever with them. One of the newer additions to these well-established pet snakes is the Andean milk snake, *Lampropeltis trian-gulum andesiana* (pictured here), a subspecies of the milk snake that nears a 6-foot length when adult.